Autonomous Vehicle Technology

A Guide for Policymakers

James M. Anderson, Nidhi Kalra, Karlyn D. Stanley, Paul Sorensen, Constantine Samaras, Oluwatobi A. Oluwatola

For more information on this publication, visit www.rand.org/t/rr443-2

This revised edition incorporates minor editorial changes.

Library of Congress Cataloging-in-Publication Data is available for this publication.

ISBN: 978-0-8330-8398-2

Published by the RAND Corporation, Santa Monica, Calif.

© Copyright 2016 RAND Corporation

RAND® is a registered trademark.

Cover image: Advertisement from 1957 for "America's Independent Electric Light and Power Companies" (art by H. Miller). Text with original: "ELECTRICITY MAY BE THE DRIVER. One day your car may speed along an electric super-highway, its speed and steering automatically controlled by electronic devices embedded in the road. Highways will be made safe—by electricity! No traffic jams…no collisions…no driver fatigue."

Preface

This report builds on RAND's long tradition of research on advanced technologies. From our research on world-circling spaceships in 1946 to developing the conceptual foundations of the Internet in the early 1960s, RAND has long provided policymakers with guidance about tomorrow's world. RAND's recent research on the policy effects of autonomous vehicles includes *Liability and Regulation of Autonomous Vehicle Technologies*, by Nidhi Kalra, James M. Anderson, and Martin Wachs (2009), and *The U.S. Experience with No-Fault Automobile Insurance: A Retrospective*, by James M. Anderson, Paul Heaton, and Stephen J. Carroll (2010). Both publications are available on RAND's website.

This report results from the RAND Corporation's Investment in People and Ideas program. Support for this program is provided, in part, by the generosity of RAND's donors and by the fees earned on client-funded research.

The RAND Transportation, Space, and Technology Program

The research reported here was conducted in the RAND Transportation, Space, and Technology Program, which addresses topics relating to transportation systems, space exploration, information and telecommunication technologies, nano- and biotechnologies, and other aspects of science and technology policy. Program research is supported by government agencies, foundations, and the private sector.

This program is part of RAND Justice, Infrastructure, and Environment, a division of the RAND Corporation dedicated to improving policy and decisionmaking in a wide range of policy domains, including civil and criminal justice, infrastructure protection and homeland security, transportation and energy policy, and environmental and natural resource policy.

Questions or comments about this report should be sent to the project leader, James Anderson, James_Anderson@rand.org. For more information about the Transportation, Space, and Technology Program, see http://www.rand.org/transportation or contact the director at tst@rand.org.

This version of the report, RR-443-2, replaces an earlier version that contained an incomplete account of General Motor's policy on its use of OnStar customer data in footnote 8 on page 69, none of which affected the findings of the report.

Contents

CHAPTER SEVEN
Liability Implications of Autonomous Vehicle Technology 111

CHAPTER EIGHT
Guidance for Policymakers and Conclusion 135

Figures and Tables

Summary

Autonomous vehicle (AV) technology offers the possibility of fundamentally changing transportation. Equipping cars and light vehicles with this technology will likely reduce crashes, energy consumption, and pollution—and reduce the costs of congestion.

This technology is most easily conceptualized using a five-part continuum suggested by the National Highway Traffic Safety Administration (NHTSA), with different benefits of the technology realized at different levels of automation:

- **Level 0:** The human driver is in complete control of all functions of the car.
- **Level 1:** One function is automated.
- **Level 2:** More than one function is automated at the same time (e.g., steering and acceleration), but the driver must remain constantly attentive.
- **Level 3:** The driving functions are sufficiently automated that the driver can safely engage in other activities.
- **Level 4:** The car can drive itself without a human driver.

Careful policymaking will be necessary to maximize the social benefits that this technology will enable, while minimizing the disadvantages. Yet policymakers are only beginning to think about the challenges and opportunities this technology poses. The goal of this report is to assist policymakers at the state and federal levels to make wise policy decisions in this rapidly evolving area.

Promise and Perils of Autonomous Vehicle Technology

AV technology has the potential to substantially affect safety, congestion, energy use, and, ultimately, land use.

Conventional driving imposes not only costs borne by the driver (e.g., fuel, depreciation, insurance), but also substantial external costs, or "negative externalities," on other people. For example, every additional driver increases congestion for all other drivers and increases the chance that another driver will have an accident. These externalities have been estimated at approximately 13 cents per mile. If a hypothetical driver drives 10,000 miles, she imposes $1,300 worth of costs on others, in addition to the costs she bears herself. AV technology has the potential to substantially reduce both the costs borne by the driver and these negative externalities, as we discuss below.

Effect on Crashes

While the frequency of crashes has been gradually declining in the United States, such incidents remain a major public health problem. There were more than 5.3 million automobile crashes in the United States in 2011, resulting in more than 2.2 million injuries and 32,000 fatalities, as well as billions of dollars in private and social costs. Worldwide, the figures are much higher.

AV technology can dramatically reduce the frequency of crashes. The Insurance Institute for Highway Safety (IIHS) estimated that if all vehicles had forward collision and lane departure warning systems, sideview (blind spot) assist, and adaptive headlights, nearly a third of crashes and fatalities could be prevented (IIHS, 2010). Automatic braking when the car detects an obstacle will also likely reduce a significant number of rear-end collisions. Technologies that permit the car to be primarily responsible for driving (Level 4) will likely further reduce crash statistics because driver error is responsible for a large proportion of crashes. This is particularly true given that 39 percent of the crash fatalities in 2011 involved alcohol use by one of the drivers. The overall social welfare benefits of vehicles that crash less frequently are significant, both for the United States and globally, and many of these benefits will go to those other purchasers of the autonomous vehicles.

Effect on Mobility

AV technology will also increase mobility for those who are currently unable or unwilling to drive. Level 4 AV technology, when the vehicle does not require a human driver, would enable transportation for the blind, disabled, or those too young to drive. The benefits for these groups would include independence, reduction in social isolation, and access to essential services. Some of these services are currently provided by mass transit or paratransit agencies, but each of these alternatives has significant disadvantages. Mass transit generally requires fixed routes that may not serve people where they live and work. Paratransit services are expensive because they require a trained, salaried, human driver. Since these costs are generally borne by taxpayers, substituting less expensive AVs for paratransit services has the potential to improve social welfare.

Effect on Traffic Congestion and Its Costs

AV technology of Level 3 or higher is likely to substantially reduce the *cost* of congestion, since occupants of vehicles could undertake other activities. These reductions to the costs of congestion will benefit individual AV operators. On the other hand, reductions or increases in congestion itself are externalities that will affect all road users. A decreased cost of driving may lead to an increase in overall vehicle miles traveled (VMT), potentially increasing actual congestion, but the technology can also enable increased throughput on roads because of more-efficient vehicle operation and reduced delays from crashes. Thus, the overall effect of AV technology on congestion is uncertain.

Land Use

As already noted, AV technology of Level 3 or above will likely decrease the cost of time in a car because the driver will be able to engage in alternative activities. Another effect of this may be to increase commuter willingness to travel longer distances to and from work. This might cause people to locate further from the urban core. Just as the rise of the automobile led to the emergence of suburbs and exurbs, so the introduction of AVs could lead to more dispersed and low-density patterns of land use surrounding metropolitan regions.

In metropolitan areas, however, it may lead to increased density as a result of the decreased need for proximate parking. One recent estimate concluded that approximately 31 percent of space in the central business districts of 41 major cities was devoted to parking (Shoup, 2005). At Level 4, an AV could simply drop its passenger off and drive away to satellite parking areas. Another consideration is that AV-sharing programs may decrease the rate of car ownership. In either event, fewer parking spaces would be necessary and would permit greater development of cities.

AV technology may have different effects on land use in the developing world. Countries with limited existing vehicle infrastructure could "leapfrog" to AV technology. Just as mobile phones allowed developing countries to skip the development of expensive landline infrastructure, AV technology might permit countries to skip some aspects of conventional, human-driver centered travel infrastructure.

Effect on Energy and Emissions

The overall effect of AV technology on energy use and pollution is uncertain, but seems likely to decrease both.

First, AV technology can improve fuel economy, improving it by 4–10 percent by accelerating and decelerating more smoothly than a human driver. Further improvements could be had from reducing distance between vehicles and increasing roadway capacity. A platoon of closely spaced AVs that stops or slows down less often resembles a train, enabling lower peak speeds (improving fuel economy) but higher effective speeds (improving travel time). Over time, as the frequency of crashes is reduced, cars and trucks could be made much lighter. This would increase fuel economy even more.

AVs might reduce pollution by enabling the use of alternative fuels. If the decrease in frequency of crashes allows lighter vehicles, many of the range issues that have limited the use of electric and other alternative vehicles are diminished. At Level 4, when human drivers become unnecessary, the vehicle could drop its owners off at a destination and then recharge or refuel on its own. One of the disadvantages of vehicles powered by electricity or fuel cells is the lack of a refueling/ recharging infrastructure. The ability of Level 4 AVs to drive and refuel themselves would permit a viable system with fewer refueling stations than would otherwise be required.

On the other hand, decreases in the cost of driving, and additions to the pool of vehicle users (e.g., elderly, disabled, and those under 16) are likely to result in an increase in overall VMT. While it seems likely that the decline in fuel consumption and emissions would outweigh any such increase, it is uncertain.

Costs

While AV technology offers the potential of substantial benefits, there are also important costs. Ironically, many of the costs of AV technology stem in part from its benefits.

For example, since AV technology is likely to decrease the cost of congestion and increase fuel economy, it will also likely decrease the private cost of driving that a particular user incurs. Because of this decline (and because of the increase in mobility that AVs offer to the elderly or disabled), AV technology may increase total VMT, which in turn may lead to increases in the negative externalities of driving, including congestion and an increase in overall fuel consumption.

AV technologies may also disrupt existing institutions. By making proximate parking unnecessary, Level 4 AV technology may undermine the parking revenues that are an important and reliable source of funding to many cities. By providing a new level of mobility to some users, it may siphon riders (and support) from public transit systems. Currently, one of the key attractions of public transit is riders' ability to undertake other tasks in transit. Autonomous vehicle technology may erode this comparative advantage.

Further, many jobs could be lost once drivers become unnecessary. Taxi, truck, and bus drivers may lose their livelihoods and professions. If crashes decline in frequency, an entire "crash economy" of insurance companies, body shops, chiropractors, and others will be disrupted.

Overall, we think the benefits of AV technology—including decreased crashes, increased mobility, and increases in fuel economy—outweigh the likely disadvantages and costs. However, further research would be useful, to more precisely estimate these costs and benefits and whether they accrue to the individual operator of the AV or the public more generally. Such research would also be helpful in determining the optimal mixture of subsidies and taxes to help align the private and public costs and benefits of this technology.

Current State Law

A number of states, including Nevada, Florida, Michigan, and California (as well as Washington, D.C.), have passed varying legislation regulating the use of AV technology. Measures have also been proposed in a number of other states.

The disadvantage of this approach is that it may create a patchwork of conflicting regulatory requirements. It is also unclear whether such measures are necessary, given the absence of commercially available vehicles with this technology and the absence of reported problems to date with the use of this technology on public roads. On the other hand, these proposals begin the conversations among the legislature, the public, and state regulatory agencies about this important and coming change in transportation.

Brief History and Current State of Autonomous Vehicles

While futurists have envisioned vehicles that drive themselves for decades, research into AV technology can be divided into three phases.

From approximately 1980 to 2003, university research centers worked on two visions of vehicle automation. The first were automated highways systems where relatively "dumb" vehicles relied on highway infrastructure to guide them. Other groups worked on AVs that did not require special roads.

From 2003 to 2007, the U.S. Defense Advanced Research Projects Agency (DARPA) held three "Grand Challenges" that markedly accelerated advancements in AV technology. The first two were held in rural environments, while the third took place in an urban environment. Each of these spurred university teams to develop the technology.

More recently, private companies have advanced AVs. Google's Driverless Car initiative has developed and tested a fleet of cars and initiated campaigns to demonstrate the applications of the technology—for example, through videos highlighting mobility offered to the blind (Google, 2012). In 2013, Audi and Toyota both unveiled their AV visions and research programs at the International Consumer Electronics Show, an annual event held every January in Las Vegas (Hsu, 2013). Nissan has also recently announced plans to sell an AV by 2020.

Current State of Technology

Google's vehicles, operating fully autonomously, have driven more than 500,000 miles without a crash attributable to the automation. Advanced sensors to gather information about the world, increasingly sophisticated algorithms to process sensor data and control the vehicle, and computational power to run them in real time has permitted this level of development.

In general, robotic systems, including AVs, use a "sense-plan-act" design. In order to sense the environment, AVs use a combination of sensors, including lidar (light detection and ranging), radar, cameras, ultrasonic, and infrared. A suite of sensors in combination can complement one another and make up for any weaknesses in any one kind of sensor. While robotic systems are very good at collecting data about the environment, making sense of that data remains probably the hardest part of developing an ultra-reliable AV.

For localization, the vehicles can use a combination of the Global Positioning System (GPS) and inertial navigation systems (INS). Challenges remain here, as well, because these systems can be somewhat inaccurate in certain conditions. For example, error of up to a meter can occur in a 10-second period during which the system relies on INS. At this point, it is not clear what combination of sensors is likely to emerge as the best combination of functionality and price—particularly for vehicles that function at Level 3 and higher.

In order to permit autonomous operation without an alert backup driver at the ready, the technology will need to degrade gracefully, in such a way that a catastrophe is avoided. For example, if some element of the system fails in the middle of a curve in busy traffic, there must be a sufficiently robust back-up system so that even with the failure, the vehicle can maneuver to a safe stop. Developing this level of reliability is challenging.

The role of vehicle to vehicle (V2V) and vehicle to infrastructure (V2I) communication in enabling AV operation also remains unclear. While this technology could ease the task of automated driving in many circumstances, it is not clear that it is necessary. Moreover, V2I might require substantial infrastructure investments—for example, if every traffic signal must be equipped with a radio for communicating with cars.

Partly as a result of all of these challenges, most (but not all) stakeholders anticipate that a "shared driving" concept will be used on the first commercially available AVs: Vehicles can drive autonomously in certain operating conditions—e.g., below a particular speed, only on certain kinds of roads, in certain driving conditions—and will revert to traditional, manual driving outside those boundaries or at the request of a human driver.

Human driver reengagement will pose another key challenge. To experience the greatest benefits of the technology, human drivers will need to be able to engage in other tasks while the vehicle is driving autonomously. For safety, however, they will need to quickly reengage (in a matter of seconds or less) at the vehicle's request. Cognitive science research on distracted driving suggests this may be a significant safety challenge. Similarly, developing the appropriate mental models for human-machine collaboration may be a challenge for a technology widely available to the public.

Software upgrades also could pose challenges, as they might need to be backward-compatible with earlier models of vehicles and sensor systems. Moreover, as more vehicle models offer autonomous driving features, software and other system upgrades will have to perform on increasingly diverse platforms, making reliability and quality assurance all the more challenging. System security is also a concern, so that viruses or malware are prevented from subverting proper functioning of vehicles' systems.

State transportation departments may need to anticipate the use of vastly different kinds of AVs operating on roadways. This may pose challenges for the registration and requirements necessary for the vehicles to operate and for the level of training particular operators must have. One short-term action that might improve safety is requiring stricter conformance to road signage requirements, particularly those that involve construction or some alteration to the roadway. This would both aid human drivers and ease some of the perception requirements for AVs.

Role of Telematics and Communications

The transfer of data to and from moving vehicles is expected to play an important role in the development of AVs in several ways. First, vehicles may use cloud-based resources. For example, AVs may use continually updated "maps" that rely in part upon sensor data from other vehicles. Similarly, if one vehicle's sensors were to malfunction it might be able to partly rely upon another vehicle's sensors. Secondly, the federal government has supported the development of Dedicated Short-Range Communications (DSRC) applications that would allow V2V and V2I communications and has reserved electromagnetic spectrum for this use. Third, nearly every stakeholder with whom we spoke noted the inevitable need for software updates, which will require some form of communications. Finally, many stakeholders believe that increasingly sophisticated "infotainment" content may occupy vehicle occupants when full-time driving is no longer necessary, and that this content may increase demand for AV technology.

A central ongoing policy issue is the future of DSRC. While DSRC licenses became available in 2004, they have only been used in experimental and demonstration projects. Recently, the Federal Communications Commission (FCC) announced in a Notice of Proposed Rulemaking that it was considering allowing unlicensed devices to share the spectrum allocated to DSRC for purposes unrelated to transportation use. We interviewed numerous stakeholders who thought this might impede the development of AVs, despite the current lack of use of the spectrum allocated to DSRC.

Other communications policy issues include the need to update distracted driver laws and the need to harmonize developmental standards for communications platforms within automobiles, along with issues pertaining to data security, data ownership, and privacy.

Standards and Regulations

Government regulations and engineering standards are policy instruments used to address safety, health, environment, and other public concerns. *Regulations* are mandatory requirements developed by policymakers that are specified by law and are enforceable by the government. *Standards*, in contrast, are engineering criteria developed by the technology community that specify how a product should be designed or how it should perform.

Both standards and regulations will play important roles in the emergence and development of AV technology.

NHTSA is the primary federal regulator of safety, and typically enacts Federal Motor Vehicle Safety Standards (FMVSSs) that specify performance standards for a wide range of safety components, including specific crash test performance. NHTSA can also issue recalls and influence the marketplace through its New Car Assessment Program. However, it has no jurisdiction over the operation of cars, actions of vehicle owners, maintenance, repair, or modifications vehicle owners may make.

Voluntary standards are also likely to play an important role in standardizing safety, assuring system compatibility, and easing some of the complex human-computer interaction problems by standardizing methods by which vehicles operate.

Liability Implications of Autonomous Vehicle Technology

The existing liability regime does not seem to present unusual concerns for owners or drivers of vehicles equipped with AV technologies. On the contrary, the decreased number of crashes and associated lower insurance costs that these technologies are expected to bring about will encourage drivers and automobile-insurance companies to adopt these technologies.

In contrast, manufacturers' product liability may increase, which could lead to inefficient delays in adoption of this technology. Manufacturers may be held responsible under several theories of liability: Warnings and consumer education will play a crucial role in managing manufacturer liability for these systems, but concerns still may slow the introduction of technologies likely to increase that liability, even if they are socially desirable.

One potential solution to this problem is to more fully integrate a cost-benefit analysis into the standard for liability in a way that accounts for consideration of the associated benefits. It is difficult to specify the appropriate sets of costs and benefits that should be considered, however, and further research would be helpful.

Manufacturers might be able to reduce these risks by changing the business model of vehicle manufacturing—e.g., offering the use of an automobile as a service rather than a product. Another approach would be for manufacturers to use technology for closer monitoring of driver behavior.

Policymakers could also take actions to reduce manufacturers' liability. Congress could explicitly preempt state tort law remedies, an approach that has some precedents. Congress could also create a reinsurance insurance backstop, if manufacturers have trouble obtaining insurance for these risks. Finally, policymakers (including the courts) could adopt an irrebuttable presumption of human control of a vehicle, to preserve the existing convention that a human driver is legally responsible for a vehicle. However, each of these approaches also has significant disadvantages and it is unclear whether any liability limitation is necessary.

Guidance for Policymakers and Conclusion

A key overarching issue for policymakers is the extent to which the positive externalities created by AV technologies will create a market failure. As detailed above, this technology has the potential to substantially benefit social welfare through its reduction of crashes and costs of congestion, declines in fuel consumption and emission, increases in mobility, and, eventually, changes to land use. Some of these potential benefits will not accrue to the purchaser of the vehicle with this technology, but more generally to the public. Since they do not accrue to the purchaser, these positive externalities will not be incorporated in the economic demand for the technology. Similarly, negative externalities—including congestion—may be caused by additional VMT. The result may be a less than socially optimal outcome. A combination of subsidies and taxes might be useful to internalize these externalities, but we currently lack the knowledge to specify them.

Overregulation also poses risks. Different states' attempts to regulate AV technology could result in a crazy quilt of incompatible requirements and regulations that would make it impossible to operate a vehicle with this technology in multiple states.

Historically, vehicle performance is tested federally by NHTSA, while driver performance is tested by state departments. Since an AV is the driver, but the human may be required to intervene in certain ways and under certain circumstances, this division of roles could become complicated.

Liability concerns may also slow the introduction of this technology. These might be addressed by a variety of policymaker approaches, including tort preemption, a federal insurance backstop, the incorporation of a long-term cost-benefit analysis in the legal standard for reasonableness, or an approach that continues to assign liability to the human operator of the vehicle.

Overall, the guiding principle for policymakers should be that AV technology ought to be permitted if and when it is superior to average human drivers. For example, safety regulations and liability rules should be designed with this overarching guiding principle in mind. Similarly, this principle can provide some guidance to judges struggling with whether a particular design decision was reasonable in the context of a products liability lawsuit.

AV technology has considerable promise for improving social welfare but will require careful policymaking at the state and federal level to maximize its promise. Policymaker intervention to align the private and public costs of this technology may be justified once its costs and benefits are better known. Further research and experience can help us better understand these uncertainties. But at this point, aggressive policymaker intervention is premature and would probably do more harm than good.

Acknowledgments

We would like to acknowledge Martin Wachs and Johanna Zmud for their helpful advice and support at the outset of this project. We also thank RAND for creating a remarkably congenial research environment and financially supporting this research. We are likewise grateful to Susan Marquis and Dick Neu for helpful suggestions over the course of the project, and to the many industry interviewees that provided us their insight on this topic. We would also like to thank the participants at the Transportation Research Board's July 2013 workshop on the Challenges and Opportunities of Road Vehicle Automation. We would also like to thank Richard Mason of RAND and Professor Ata Khan of Carleton University for their helpful reviews and comments.

James Anderson would like to thank Sarah Hauer for her numerous edits and help with countless logistical details over the life of this project. He also thanks Katherine Brownlee, Sarah Anderson-Brownlee, and Hannah Anderson-Brownlee for their helpful suggestions about autonomous vehicles, and Matthew Anderson-Brownlee for his enthusiasm for automation of all kinds. He would also like to credit Guido Calabresi's *The Costs of Accidents* (1970) for his interest in traffic safety.

Abbreviations

ACC	adaptive cruise control
ALI	American Law Institute
AV	autonomous vehicle
BTS	Bureau of Transportation Statistics
CAFE	Corporate Average Fuel Economy
Caltrans	California Department of Transportation
CO_2	carbon dioxide
CWS	collision warning system
DARPA	U.S. Defense Advanced Research Projects Agency
DMV	department of motor vehicles
DOT	department of transportation
DSRC	Dedicated Short-Range Communications
EDR	Event Data Recorder
EPA	U.S. Environmental Protection Agency
FCC	Federal Communications Commission
FHWA	Federal Highway Administration
FMVSS	Federal Motor Vehicle Safety Standard
GHG	greenhouse gas
GHz	gigahertz
GPS	Global Positioning System
GSM	Global System for Mobile Communications

GREET	Greenhouse Gases, Regulated Emissions, and Energy Use in Transportation
IHRA-ITS	International Harmonized Research Activities working group on intelligent transport systems
IIHS	Insurance Institute for Highway Safety
INS	inertial navigation systems
ISO	International Organization for Standardization
ITS America	Intelligent Transportation Society of America
kWh	kilowatt-hours
LTE	Long Term Evolution
MHz	megahertz
mpg	miles per gallon
mph	miles per hour
NDMV	Nevada Department of Motor Vehicles
NHTSA	National Highway Traffic Safety Administration
NPRM	Notice of Proposed Rulemaking
NRC	National Research Council
NTIA	National Telecommunications and Information Agency
NTSB	National Transportation Safety Board
OEM	original equipment manufacturer
RITA	Research and Innovative Technology Administration
SAE	Society of Automotive Engineers
U-NII	Unlicensed National Information Infrastructure
V2I	vehicle to infrastructure
V2V	vehicle to vehicle
VIN	vehicle identification number
VMT	vehicle miles traveled

CHAPTER ONE

Introduction

The General Motors *Futurama* exhibit presented at the 1939 World's Fair in New York piqued the collective American and world imagination. Among other wonders, it promised that the United States would have an automated highway system and foretold the coming of a fundamental revolution in the surface transportation of passengers and freight. Today, nearly 75 years later, the advances in autonomous vehicle (AV) technology (also known as automated driving systems) place us on the cusp of that revolution.

AVs have enormous potential to allow for more productive use of time spent in a vehicle and to reduce crashes, costs of congestion, energy consumption, and pollution. They may also alter models of vehicle ownership and patterns of land use, and may create new markets and economic opportunities. Yet policymakers are only beginning to grapple with the immense changes AVs portend. They face many policy questions, the answers to which will be influential in shaping the adoption and impact of AVs. These include everything from when and whether this technology should be permitted on the roads to the appropriate liability regime. This report seeks to aid policymakers by summarizing a large body of knowledge relevant to these policy issues, and suggesting appropriate policy principles.

Our methodology was straightforward. We conducted a comprehensive literature review of the work on AV technologies and formally interviewed approximately 30 stakeholders—including automobile manufacturers; technology firms; communications providers; representatives from National Highway Traffic Safety Administration

(NHTSA), state departments of transportation (DOTs), state departments of motor vehicles (DMVs), and others. (A summary of the interviews is included in the appendix.) We talked to many others at the Transportation Research Board Annual Meeting and the Transportation Research Board's Workshop on Road Vehicle Automation.

In the remainder of this chapter, we briefly define different levels of vehicle autonomy, explore why they merit the attention of policymakers, and enumerate questions that policymakers will need to address.

What Are Autonomous and Automated Vehicles?

Technological advancements are creating a continuum between conventional, fully human-driven vehicles and AVs, which partially or fully drive themselves and which may ultimately require no driver at all. Within this continuum are technologies that enable a vehicle to assist and make decisions for a human driver. Such technologies include crash warning systems, adaptive cruise control (ACC), lane keeping systems, and self-parking technology.[1]

NHTSA has created a five-level hierarchy to help clarify this continuum.[2] We summarize this below and use it throughout this report:

- **Level 0 (no automation):** The driver is in complete and sole control of the primary vehicle functions (brake, steering, throttle, and motive power) at all times, and is solely responsible for monitoring the roadway and for safe vehicle operation.
- **Level 1 (function-specific automation):** Automation at this level involves one or more specific control functions; if multiple functions are automated, they operate independently of each other. The driver has overall control, and is solely responsible for safe operation, but can choose to cede limited authority over a pri-

---

[1]   These technologies are sometimes called advanced driver assistance systems.

[2]   The Society of Automotive Engineers (SAE) International has created a somewhat similar taxonomy to describe automation for on-road vehicles (SAE On-Road Automated Vehicle Standards Committee, 2013).

mary control (as in ACC); the vehicle can automatically assume limited authority over a primary control (as in electronic stability control); or the automated system can provide added control to aid the driver in certain normal driving or crash-imminent situations (e.g., dynamic brake support in emergencies).

- **Level 2 (combined-function automation):** This level involves automation of at least two primary control functions designed to work in unison to relieve the driver of controlling those functions. Vehicles at this level of automation can utilize shared authority when the driver cedes active primary control in certain limited driving situations. The driver is still responsible for monitoring the roadway and safe operation, and is expected to be available for control at all times and on short notice. The system can relinquish control with no advance warning and the driver must be ready to control the vehicle safely.

- **Level 3 (limited self-driving automation):** Vehicles at this level of automation enable the driver to cede full control of all safety-critical functions under certain traffic or environmental conditions, and in those conditions to rely heavily on the vehicle to monitor for changes in those conditions requiring transition back to driver control. The driver is expected to be available for occasional control, but with sufficiently comfortable transition time.

- **Level 4 (full self-driving automation):** The vehicle is designed to perform all safety-critical driving functions and monitor roadway conditions for an entire trip. Such a design anticipates that the driver will provide destination or navigation input, but is not expected to be available for control at any time during the trip. This includes both occupied and unoccupied vehicles. By design, safe operation rests solely on the automated vehicle system. (NHTSA, 2013).

The type and magnitude of the potential benefits of AV technology will depend on the level of automation that is achieved. For example, some of the safety benefits of AV technology may be achieved from function-specific automation (e.g., automatic braking), while the land-use and environmental benefits are likely to be realized only by full automation (Level 4).[3]

Why Is Autonomous Vehicle Technology Important Now?

AV technology merits the immediate attention of policymakers for several reasons. First, the technology appears close to maturity and commercial introduction. Google's efforts—which involve a fleet of cars that collectively have logged hundreds of thousands of autonomous miles—have received widespread media attention and demonstrate that this technology has advanced considerably. Every major commercial automaker is engaged in research in this area and full-scale commercial introduction of truly autonomous (including driverless) vehicles are being predicted to occur within five to 20 years. Several states have passed laws to regulate the use of AVs, and many more laws have been proposed. As these technologies trickle (or flood) into the marketplace, it is important for both state and federal policymakers to understand the effects that existing policy (or lack thereof) are likely to have on the development and adoption of this technology.

Second, the stakes are high. In the United States alone, more than 30,000 people are killed each year in crashes, approximately 2.5 million are injured, and the vast majority of these crashes are the result of human error (Choi et al., 2008). By greatly reducing the opportunity for human error, AV technologies have the potential to greatly reduce the number of crashes.[4]

---

[3]   AV technology is closely related to, but distinct from, connected vehicle technology, which enables the vehicle to share information with other vehicles or transportation infrastructure. For example, cars could share location information electronically with nearby vehicles, which could aid AVs. More ambitiously, cars might share sensor information with nearby vehicles, which could provide an AV with more information on which to base its decisionmaking. While some have argued that connected vehicle technology will be central to achieving AV operation (KPMG and Center for Automotive Research, 2012), this view is not universally shared and many of our interviewees believe that sensor-based systems will be sufficient. We discuss connected vehicle technology in Chapter Four.

[4]   Similarly, a study of commercial vehicles found that a bundled system of collision warning, ACC, and advanced braking could prevent 23–28 percent of rear-end crashes (Batelle, 2007).

AVs may also reduce congestion and its associated costs. Estimates suggest that effective road capacity (vehicles per lane per hour) can be doubled or tripled. The costs of congestion can also be greatly reduced if vehicle operators can productively conduct other work. AV technology also promises to reduce energy use.[5] Automobiles have become increasingly heavy over the past 20 years partly to meet more rigorous crash test standards. If crashes become exceedingly rare events, it may be possible to dramatically lighten automobiles.

In the long run, AVs may also improve land use. Quite apart from the environmental toll of fuel generation and consumption, the existing automobile shapes much of our built environment. Its centrality to our lives accounts for the acres of parking in even our most densely occupied cities.[6] With the ability to drive and park themselves at some distance from their users, AVs may obviate the need for nearby parking for commercial, residential, or work establishments, which may enable a reshaping of the urban environment and permit new in-fill development as adjacent parking lots are made unnecessary.

Along with these benefits, however, AVs could have many negative effects. By reducing the time cost of driving, AVs may encourage greater travel and increase total vehicle miles traveled (VMT), which could lead to more congestion.[7] They may increase sprawl if commuters move ever farther away from workplaces. Similarly, AVs may eventually

---

[5] One study found that "because [adaptive cruise control] reduces the degree of acceleration relative to manual driving, and because [adaptive cruise control] would be used more than [conventional cruise control], deployment of [adaptive cruise control] systems will result in increased fuel efficiency and decreased emissions" (Koziol et al., 1999, pp. 5–17).

[6] Anticipating the future importance of the car, modernist architect Le Corbusier famously designed the ground floor of La Villa Savoye in 1928 to mirror the turning radius of the owners' car (a 1927 Citroen) (Kroll, 2010).

[7] The U.S. DOT Highway Economic Requirements System (HERS) estimates vehicle-demand price elasticity in the most likely scenarios to fall by −0.7 to −0.8 in the short run, and to fall about twice that in the long run, with a range of −1.0 to −2.0 (Lee, Klein, and Camus, 1999; Litman, 2012). This implies that as travel costs (time and expenses) reduce by 10 percent, travel is expected to increase: by 7 to 8 percent in the short run (time period over which exogenous demand factors remain fixed, probably about one year) and by an additional 2 to 12 percent in the long run (time for exogenous characteristics to change, frequently assumed at five to 20 years).

shift users' preferences toward larger vehicles to permit other activities. In theory, this could even include beds, showers, kitchens, or offices. If AV software becomes standardized, a single flaw might lead to many accidents. Internet-connected systems might be hacked by the malicious. And perhaps the biggest risks are simply unknowable.

From seatbelts, to air bags, to antilock brakes, automakers have often been reluctant to incorporate expensive new technology, even if it can save many lives (Mashaw and Harfst, 1990). Navigating the AV landscape makes implementation of these earlier safety improvements appear simple by comparison. Negotiating the risks to reach the opportunities will require careful policymaking, and this report identifies the critical issues and context as policymakers collectively define a path forward.

What Decisions Do Policymakers Face?

Policymakers have a number of opportunities for shaping the adoption and impact of AV technologies. Key questions include:

- How, if at all, should the use of AVs be regulated, and at what level?
- What kinds of vehicles should be allowed on the road, and who is allowed to operate them?
- How should the safety of AVs be tested, and by whom? To what safety standards should AVs be held?
- How might different liability regimes shape the timely and safe adoption of AVs, and what are the tradeoffs? Under what conditions would limitations on tort liability be appropriate?
- What are the implications of a patchwork of state-by-state laws and regulations, and what are the tradeoffs in harmonizing these policies?
- To what extent should policymakers encourage the adoption of AVs; e.g., through smart road infrastructure, dedicated highway lanes, manufacturer or consumer incentives?

Different policymaking bodies will have different roles in addressing these questions. In recent years, state legislatures have passed laws on what types of AVs may be driven, and have directed DMVs to clarify testing and regulation procedures. Legislatures may also be responsible for providing specific incentives for manufacturers to create AVs and for the public to adopt them. Historically, DMVs test the safety of and regulate drivers (i.e., issuing driver's licenses), while federal bodies like NHTSA regulate and test the safety of vehicles. AVs blur the line between vehicle and driver, and DMVs are beginning to test and license AVs. State DOTs maintain and operate highway infrastructure, and thus would be responsible for any investments in intelligent infrastructure or the creation and operation of dedicated lanes for AVs.

The goal of this report is to summarize available information on AV technologies, identify the most salient policy issues, and provide tentative guidance to policymakers. At the outset, we must note that there are far more questions than answers. Further research can and should be conducted on almost every topic we touch.

The remainder of the report is organized as follows. Chapter Two summarizes the potential of these technologies to improve social welfare and potential detrimental effects. Chapter Three summarizes recent state legislation in this area. In Chapter Four, we review the history of AV technology and discuss its current status. In Chapter Five, we address the particular policy issues raised by telematics and communications issues. In Chapter Six, we address the role of standards and regulations. In Chapter Seven, we discuss the liability implications of AV technology and the risks that are raised to the goal of maximizing social welfare. Chapter Eight summarizes the policy implications of this work and proposes some tentative suggestions. We also summarize our findings and propose directions for further research in this area.

CHAPTER TWO

The Promise and Perils of Autonomous Vehicle Technology

AVs have the potential to substantially affect safety, mobility, congestion, land use, and the environment. In this chapter, we discuss some of the social costs of transportation and how AVs could affect these costs. In general, we find that AV technology has the potential to substantially reduce many of the existing negative externalities of personal automobile use and create some additional benefits in increased mobility and improving land use. While there are some important disadvantages, we find these are generally outweighed by the advantages.

However, the extent to which the specific benefit accrues to the purchaser of the car, rather than the public as a whole, varies by the benefit. For example, the extent to which this technology can reduce the cost of congestion (by allowing a driver to attend to other tasks) will accrue to the driver. On the other hand, the extent to which the technology can generally reduce congestion on the roads accrues to the general motoring public, not the purchaser. This is important because it will affect the business model for the introduction of many of these technologies, and whether subsidies or taxes are appropriate to align private and public costs.

A Summary of the Social Costs of Driving

There is a large body of research estimating the social costs (or externalities) of human-driven vehicles (e.g., Small and Kazimi, 1995; Delucchi, 2000; Parry, Wells, and Harrington, 2007; Michalek et al.,

2011). These externalities include accidents, congestion, noise, air pollution, and greenhouse gas (GHG) emissions. Traffic accidents, for example, are the leading cause of death among young adults 15–29 years old, and the second-highest cause of death for children 5–14 years old (World Health Organization, 2013). Traffic accidents have other social and individual costs, including property damage; lost earnings; lost household production; medical costs; emergency services; vocational rehabilitation; workplace costs; administrative costs; legal costs; and pain, suffering, and lost quality of life. NHTSA estimated in a 2002 study that the total economic cost of motor vehicle crashes in 2000 was a staggering $230.6 billion (Blincoe et al., 2002).

There are also estimates of the external costs of noise, congestion, air pollution, oil imports, and GHG emissions. NHTSA estimated these costs in its Final Regulatory Impact Analysis report (2012a), which examines the costs and benefits of increasing the Corporate Average Fuel Economy (CAFE) standards for vehicles manufactured between 2017 and 2025. Table 2.1 shows some of these cost estimates.

Environmental damage, such as GHG emissions and air pollution, is another important externality of driving that could be affected by autonomous driving. GHG emissions have social costs relating to

Table 2.1
Estimates of External Costs of Driving (2010$)

Mobility Costs ($/Vehicle-Mile)	External Costs from Automobile Use	External Costs from Light-Truck Use
Congestion	0.056	0.050
Accidents	0.024	0.027
Noise	0.001	0.001
Emissions Cost	**Weighted Costs**	
Volatile organic compounds (VOC)	$1,700/ton	
Nitrogen oxides (NOx)	$6,700/ton	
Particulate matter ($PM_{2.5}$)	$306,500/ton	
Sulfur dioxide	$39,600/ton	
Carbon dioxide (CO_2) emissions in 2010	$22/metric ton	
Economic Benefits of Reducing Oil Imports	**$0.197/gallon in 2025**	

SOURCE: NHTSA, 2012a.

the impacts of climate change, while conventional air pollutants from gasoline and diesel combustion affect human health, crop loss, reforestation, and other areas (National Research Council [NRC], 2010).

In 2013, a U.S. interagency working group updated the estimates of the social costs of carbon dioxide (CO_2). These estimates allow agencies to incorporate the social benefits of CO_2 reduction into regulatory actions and cost-benefit analyses. The central value for the social cost of CO_2 in 2020 is about $48 per metric ton, with a range from $12 to $145 per metric ton (U.S. Interagency Working Group on Social Cost of Carbon, 2013). The U.S. Environmental Protection Agency (EPA) pegged emissions from U.S. light-duty vehicles at 1,080 million metric tons in 2011 (EPA, 2013a), so the social cost of CO_2 emissions from light-duty vehicles was nearly $41 billion annually.

Somewhat confusingly, different externalities are estimated in different ways. Impacts from air pollution, GHG emissions, and oil imports are estimated on a per-ton or a per-gallon basis. This means impacts can be reduced through vehicles that are more fuel efficient, fuels that are less emissions intensive, and fuels other than refined petroleum products. Conversely, impacts from congestion and accidents are largely a function of the amount of driving, so impacts increase when VMT increase.

So that we can compare external costs on a per-mile basis, we apply NHTSA's cost estimates to the per-mile vehicle emissions from a base case car in Argonne National Laboratory's Greenhouse Gases, Regulated Emissions, and Energy Use in Transportation (GREET) model (Argonne National Laboratory, 2012) and depict these in Figure 2.1. NHTSA's estimates in Table 2.1 and from Figure 2.1 illustrate that while environmental and oil security costs are significant, congestion and accidents are the two largest external costs of driving per mile. When gasoline costs $3.50 per gallon, the fuel costs for driving a mile in a car that gets 25 miles per gallon (mpg) are about 14 cents. The social costs estimated here add another 13 cents per mile—nearly as much as the cost to fuel the car.[1] The ability for AV technology to con-

---

[1]   Some of the externalities per mile will vary by time and location. For example, the congestion and noise costs imposed upon others will be much less than 5.6 cents a mile if the mile

Figure 2.1
An Estimate of the Per-Mile Externalities Associated with Driving an Automobile

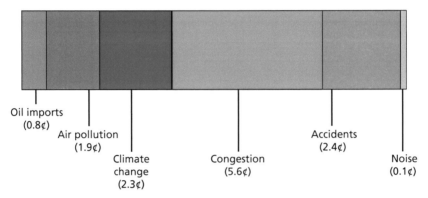

Oil imports (0.8¢)
Air pollution (1.9¢)
Climate change (2.3¢)
Congestion (5.6¢)
Accidents (2.4¢)
Noise (0.1¢)

NOTE: Estimates are in 2010$ and based on NHTSA (2012a) values. GHG emissions use the central value from the U.S. Interagency Working Group on the Social Cost of Carbon (2013). Emissions factors are well-to-wheel for a 24.8-mpg vehicle using data from Argonne National Laboratory (2012).
RAND RR443-2.1

siderably reduce these social costs not only benefits society if realized; it also has major implications for future cost-benefit analyses conducted in support of regulatory actions and policy decisions.

Having summarized the substantial social costs of human-driven vehicles, we now turn to the effects of AV technology on those social costs.

Effects of Autonomous Vehicle Technology on Safety and Crashes

In the United States in 2011, there were more than 5.3 million automobile crashes, resulting in more than 2.2 million injuries and more than 32,000 fatalities. These casualties are a public health issue, and impose

---

is on an empty road in the desert. Conversely, the congestion and noise costs will be much higher if it is in a dense city. These estimates are based on data in the United States. The pattern of externalities will be different in other countries.

billions of dollars in private and social costs. AV technology has the potential to substantially reduce this human toll.

Both in absolute numbers and on a per-VMT basis, automobile crashes have been diminishing in the United States. Total roadway crashes per million VMT, which overwhelmingly comprised light-duty vehicle crashes, fell at an annual average rate of about 2.3 percent from 1990 to 2011. Over the same period, roadway injuries fell at an average annual rate of about 3.1 percent. So the rate of injuries from crashes was reducing faster than the rate of crashes themselves—while fewer crashes were occurring, vehicles were also getting safer for their occupants. Figure 2.2 shows how total U.S. roadway crashes and injuries per million VMT have fallen. Of the more than 2 million roadway injuries in 2011, 69,000 were pedestrians and 48,000 were cyclists, demonstrating that crash risks are not limited to occupants of the vehicles.

A similar improvement was achieved in reducing U.S. roadway fatalities from 51 per billion VMT in 1960 to 11 per billion VMT in 2011, as shown in Figure 2.3. This represents an average annual decline

Figure 2.2
U.S. Roadway Accidents and Injuries per Million Vehicle Miles Traveled

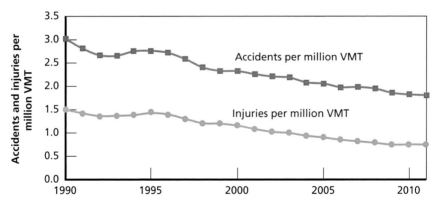

NOTE: Data from the Bureau of Transportation Statistics (BTS, 2013) includes all highway transportation modes: passenger car, light truck, motorcycle, large truck, and bus. Crashes involving two or more motor vehicles are counted as one "crash" by the U.S. DOT, so total crashes shown here are fewer than the sum of individual vehicles involved. Injuries include vehicle occupants for all highway modes as well as pedestrians and cyclists.

RAND *RR443-2.2*

Figure 2.3
U.S. Roadway Fatalities per Billion Vehicle Miles Traveled

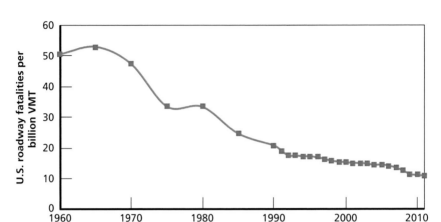

NOTE: Data from BTS (2013) includes all highway transportation modes: passenger car, light truck, motorcycle, large truck, and bus. Fatalities include vehicle occupants for all highway modes, as well as pedestrians and cyclists.
RAND RR443-2.3

in fatalities of about 2.9 percent. Still, the fact there were more than 32,000 fatalities on U.S. roadways in 2011 shows that considerable safety improvements are necessary.

Fatalities from car and light truck occupants were about 21,000 of the total fatalities; motorcycles added more than 4,600 fatalities with much fewer VMT (BTS, 2013). And, similar to the injuries discussed above, pedestrian casualties were a considerable portion of the total, more than 4,400 in 2011. So, light-duty vehicle operation poses a risk not only for other light-duty vehicle passengers, but also to motorcyclists, pedestrians, and cyclists.

Many factors contributed to reducing the rate of crashes, injuries, and fatalities—including the gradual adoption of on-vehicle safety technologies. These systems were introduced in various model years: modern frontal air bags in 1984, antilock brakes in 1985, electronic stability control in 1995, head-protecting side air bags in 1998, and forward collision warnings in 2000 (IIHS, 2012). But it typically takes three decades for safety features that start out on luxury vehicles to reach the entire vehicle fleet, as older vehicles are replaced with newer models. If the adoption of forward collision warning systems (CWSs) continues on its current path (standard on 1 percent and optional on 11 percent of model year 2010 vehicles), it could take nearly 50 years to reach 95 percent of the fleet (IIHS, 2012).

Based on the data from 1960 to 2011, the rate of fatalities has halved every two decades on U.S. roadways. It is likely that AVs could bend this fatality curve substantially. But the safety benefits will likely depend upon the level of automation.

The IIHS estimated that if all vehicles had forward collision and lane departure warning, sideview (blind spot) assist, and adaptive headlights, nearly a third of crashes and fatalities could be prevented (IIHS, 2010). These features are generally associated with Level 0 or Level 1 vehicle automation.

Dynamic brake support, a Level 1 feature, reduces stopping distances for drivers who have made a decision to stop quickly. This will improve safety outcomes, but will not cure driver error in situations where no decision is made to stop. As vehicle automation technology advances from function-specific automation (Level 1) to Combined Function Automation (Level 2), the driver can cede active primary control in some situations, and at least two functions can be automated to work in unison. For example, vehicles could perform the functions of staying in one lane and ACC, with the safety benefits of both functions likely greater than if either were to be automated individually.

Level 3 automation allows the driver to cede full control of all safety-critical functions in certain situations. Crashes, injuries, and fatalities due to driver error under this condition would likely be substantially reduced.[2] Level 3 vehicles also might drastically reduce the number of crashes, injuries, and fatalities involving motorcycles, pedestrians, and cyclists, as vehicles automated at this level will not be distracted, impaired, or reckless—and can increase avoidance of

---

[2] This is significant as more than 14,000 of the 32,000 roadway deaths in 2011 involved a single vehicle (BTS, 2013). Of course, driver error is still possible from other vehicles on the road that do not have automation features, or whose automation is not engaged.

others who might be.[3] However, Level 2 and 3 automation also might increase some categories of crashes if consumers rely upon the systems too much.

There may be further risk reductions with the transition from Level 3 to Level 4 automation, especially in the number of alcohol-related crashes. In 2011, alcohol was involved in more than 39 percent of motorist fatalities, and roadway safety could improve exponentially when these impaired drivers cede control to fully self-driving auto-mated vehicles. Eliminating up to a third of traffic deaths through vehicle automation just by limiting alcohol-impaired drivers would represent a dramatic improvement in roadway safety.

In short, we find that AV technology will likely lead to substantial reductions in crashes and the resulting human toll. While a portion of these benefits will accrue to the purchaser of the vehicle, much of the benefit is in the form of a positive externality to other vehicles, pedestrians, and bicyclists.[4]

Further research to develop more precise estimates of the private and public benefits of different specific technologies would be very useful. Such estimates might assist policymakers in conducting cost-benefit analyses and deciding whether subsidies or mandates for specific technologies are warranted.

Effect of Autonomous Vehicle Technologies on Mobility for Those Unable to Drive

Google recently released a much-watched YouTube video of its autonomous car transporting a blind man (Google, 2012). Level 4 vehicles could substantially increase access and mobility across a range of populations currently unable or not permitted to use conventional automo-

---

[3]   In 2011, 49 percent of pedestrians killed by motor vehicles were under the influence of alcohol. Similarly, 38 percent of cyclists killed by motor vehicles were under the influence of alcohol (BTS, 2013).

[4]   Consumers may also undervalue safety benefits because they believe their driving abilities are better than average and underestimate the chance that they will be in a crash.

biles. These include the disabled, older citizens, and children under the age of 16. Some benefits for this group include personal independence, reduction in social isolation, and access to essential services (e.g., Burkhardt, Berger, and McGavock, 1996; Harrison and Ragland, 2003; Rosenbloom, 2001; Rosenbloom, 2012).

Where existing public transit agencies provide services to the disabled, 14 to 18 percent of their budgets, on average, are used to provide on-demand paratransit services. The per-trip costs of these services are often three or more times those of fixed-route transit services (GAO, 2012). Level 4 automation could expand mobility and access at reduced costs. While most of this category of benefits would be provided to users of these AVs, there would also be a broader societal benefit in reducing the amount of paratransit services.

Congestion

We now consider the potential effects of AVs on traffic congestion and the associated cost implications. This discussion is somewhat speculative, as there are many factors involved with uncertain feedback relationships. On the whole, however, it appears that broad adoption of AV technology, while potentially stimulating additional vehicle travel, could lead to significant reduction in congestion and an even greater reduction in the costs associated with it.

Potential Effects on Traffic Congestion

The introduction of AVs could directly affect traffic congestion in at least three ways: influencing total VMT per capita, enabling greater vehicle throughput on existing roads, and reducing traffic delays stemming from vehicle crashes.

VMT. The potential effects of AVs on aggregate VMT remain unclear, though it seems likely they will lead to more total travel rather than less.[5] Decisions on where to live and what trips to make are mediated by travel costs, which include vehicle operating costs—

---

[5]   See Smith (2012b).

depreciation, insurance, fuel, parking, maintenance, and the like—along with the value (or opportunity cost) of a driver's time. AVs could help reduce several of these travel cost components. First, AVs would free drivers to engage in other productive or enjoyable activities—working, reading, watching a movie, or even sleeping—during a trip, thus reducing the opportunity cost of time spent in the car. Second, to the extent that AVs are able to promote smoother traffic patterns, they should lead to improved fuel economy and, in turn, lower fuel costs.[6] Third, on trips to major activity centers where parking prices are high, an AV could pilot itself to a cheaper remote lot after dropping off its passengers, thus cutting parking costs.[7] Fourth, if AVs are as successful at reducing the risk of vehicle crashes as anticipated, they could result in a significant reduction in insurance premiums.[8]

All these factors combined could significantly reduce the marginal travel costs associated with automobility. In response, many households might choose to live in more remote areas where housing is more affordable given that longer commutes and other personal trips would no longer be as onerous or as costly. The net effect of these factors, then, should be to increase total VMT.

AVs could also influence total VMT by enabling a new modality for urban travel (KPMG and Center for Automotive Research, 2012)—a driverless taxi system that over time replaces traditional taxi service, car-sharing programs, and possibly even transit lines. Driverless taxis could offer the same on-demand, door-to-door convenience

---

[6] Research indicates that per-mile fuel use and greenhouse gas emissions begin to rise rapidly as average travel speeds fall below 20 miles per hour, owing largely to the inefficient start-and-stop driving patterns that occur in heavily congested conditions (Barth and Boriboonsomsin, 2009).

[7] Apart from potentially increasing VMT by decreasing the cost of driving, remote parking would directly increase VMT because of additional travel to remote lots.

[8] While conventional auto insurance is priced as a flat rate that is relatively insensitive to changes in miles traveled, auto insurers are increasing the use of plans based on the number of miles driven. This changes insurance costs from fixed prices, incurred by the consumer no matter how much or little she drives, to variable costs, which would increase or decrease depending on miles driven.

of traditional taxis, but at far lower prices, as there would be no need to pay for a driver's time.

To consider the potential effects of driverless taxis on VMT, it is instructive to examine results from current car-sharing programs. Members can check out a vehicle for short periods of time, with fees typically based on some combination of hours of use and miles of travel (Martin and Shaheen, 2010). The ability to join a car-sharing service has led some urban households to reduce the number of vehicles owned, and others to forgo auto ownership entirely. Owning an automobile can cost thousands of dollars per year, so there is ample financial motivation for reducing auto ownership.

With car-sharing programs, members are able to save the annual fixed costs associated with traditional auto ownership, including capital depreciation, finance charges, vehicle registration fees, and insurance. These costs are instead shouldered by the car-sharing program and then passed back to members in higher per-hour or per-mile usage fees. The net effect, from the member perspective, is that the fixed costs of auto ownership are eliminated, but the marginal (per-mile or per-trip) costs are greater, and this generally leads to an overall reduction in vehicle travel.

Recent data on the cost of auto ownership and use from AAA provide insight into the financial implications of switching from auto ownership to car-sharing (AAA, 2013). According to AAA, the average fixed annual costs of owning a mid-sized sedan that is driven 10,000 miles a year, for example, come out to $5,695, including $3,244 for depreciation, $831 for finance charges, $1,020 for auto insurance, and $600 for registration and additional fees. Vehicle operating costs add another 21 cents per mile, including about 15 cents for gas, just under 5 cents for maintenance, and just over 1 cent for tires (note that the AAA data do not include the costs associated with tolls and parking, as these vary considerably from one region to the next).

Based on these numbers, a household could save about $6,000 in fixed annual costs by joining a car-sharing program rather than owning a vehicle (or a second vehicle, or a third). The underlying costs, however, would be passed back to members in the form of higher per-mile rates. Assume, for example, that the $5,695 in fixed costs is apportioned over 10,000 miles, resulting in an additional 56.9 cents per mile. Added together with the 21-cents-per-mile cost for fuel, maintenance, and tires, the per-mile cost of a car-sharing plan would then be about 77 cents per mile, almost quadruple the marginal cost of driving with auto ownership.

So, for households that opt for car-sharing as an alternative to auto ownership, the marginal or per-trip cost of driving becomes much higher, typically leading to much lower VMT. Yet car-sharing programs also include members who, prior to joining, did not own a vehicle. Any car-sharing trips taken by such members represent VMT that would not have occurred absent the ability to use car-sharing. In theory, therefore, these programs could either increase or reduce total VMT. However, based on a recent survey of car-sharing members in the United States (Martin and Shaheen, 2010), it appears that car-sharing leads to a net reduction in VMT. In other words, the reduction in VMT among members who would have otherwise chosen to own an additional vehicle is greater than the additional VMT from members who would have relied instead on transit, walking, or other alternative travel modes for all of their trips.

Returning to the question of AVs, it is quite likely that the availability of driverless taxis could likewise motivate some households to reduce levels of auto ownership; absent the need to pay for a driver's time, an autonomously piloted taxi should not cost any more than car-sharing, and would offer even greater door-to-door convenience. As with car-sharing, however, the annual fixed costs associated with auto ownership would be apportioned into the per-mile rates for using a driverless taxi, increasing the marginal cost for each trip made. Here again, this should have the overall effect of reducing VMT.

There is one important caveat. For individuals who own a vehicle and frequently park in crowded urban areas, parking fees may increase the marginal cost of each trip considerably. With a driverless taxi service, parking fees would no longer be needed (rather, the AV would simply continue on to pick up the next fare). Depending on the magnitude of parking fees in relation to the additional per-mile costs associated with depreciation, insurance, and the like, it is thus possible that reliance on driverless taxis could eliminate the fixed costs of auto ownership for a household and, at least in some cases, also reduce the marginal cost for each trip made. This would tend to promote additional VMT.

In short, AVs appear likely to reduce many of the costs typically associated with automotive travel, which likely to stimulate growth in VMT. AVs could also enable the emergence of driverless taxis, for which the ultimate effect on VMT is more uncertain.

Vehicle throughput. While AVs might lead to an increase in overall vehicle travel, they could also support higher vehicle throughput rates on existing roads. To begin with, the ability to constantly monitor surrounding traffic and respond with finely tuned braking and acceleration adjustments should enable AVs to travel safely at higher speeds and with reduced headway (space) between each vehicle. Research indicates that the platooning of AVs could increase lane capacity (vehicles per lane per hour) by up to 500 percent (Fernandez and Nunes, 2012, as cited in KPMG and Center for Automotive Research, 2012).

In more congested travel conditions, AVs could help to avoid the inefficient start-and-stop traffic conditions—a result of exaggerated braking and acceleration responses of human drivers—that lead to a severe degradation in vehicle throughput. When plotted over time, observations of highway travel speeds and traffic volumes form a backward-bending curve, as illustrated in Figure 2.4.

When there are few cars on the freeway, travel speeds are high and throughput is obviously low. As the number of cars increases, speed diminishes slightly, while total throughput continues to increase. At a certain point, however, the addition of too many vehicles triggers sharper braking responses and, in turn, the start-and-stop conditions of traffic congestion. As this occurs, both travel speed and throughput sharply diminish (Sorensen et al., 2008).

Traffic observations from State Route 91 in Southern California illustrate the degree to which traffic congestion can adversely affect vehicle throughput. The State Route 91 facility, which traverses east-west from Orange County to Riverside County, includes four general-purpose (free) lanes in each direction, along with two tolled express lanes in each direction that rely on congestion pricing (higher tolls during peak periods) to ensure free-flowing travel conditions. During

Figure 2.4
Relationship Between Roadway Speed and Roadway Throughput

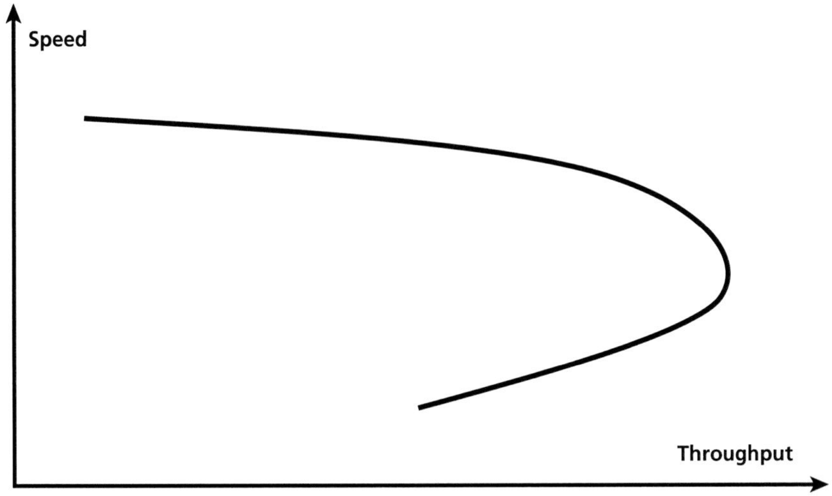

peak travel hours, traffic speeds of 60 to 65 miles per hour (mph) are maintained in the express lanes, while speeds in the adjacent general-purpose lanes slow to 15 to 20 mph. At the same time, the express lanes carry roughly double the number of vehicles per lane per hour as the congested general-purpose lanes (Obenberger, 2004).

The State Route 91 example illustrates how maintaining smoother flowing traffic conditions with congestion pricing can help prevent the significant deterioration in vehicle throughput resulting from severe traffic congestion that is suggested by the backward-bending portion of the curve in Figure 2.4. To the extent they are able to reduce start-and-stop traffic through more finely controlled braking and acceleration, AVs should have an analogous effect on maintaining higher through-put during peak travel hours.

Crash-related traffic congestion. There are two broad categories of traffic congestion: recurrent delays and nonrecurrent delays. Recur-rent delays—congestion that occurs in the same time and location on a daily basis—are the result of prevailing travel patterns in which the number of vehicles trying to use a road at the same time exceeds the road's capacity. Nonrecurrent delays, in contrast, stem from isolated events or limited-duration circumstances—such as construction, severe weather, a large sporting event, a disabled vehicle, or a traffic crash—that act to either reduce capacity or create a surge in demand. According to the Federal Highway Administration (FHWA), nonrecurrent congestion accounts for roughly half of all congestion delays (FHWA, 2013). Traffic incidents—e.g., a disabled vehicle, a minor collision, an overturned hazardous material truck—account for about half of all nonrecurrent delays. Weather is responsible for another 30 percent, and roadwork accounts for the remaining 20 percent.

Traffic incidents, then, account for about 25 percent of all congestion delays (including both recurrent and nonrecurrent congestion), and vehicle crashes constitute a major share of this total (crashes typically result in lengthier delays than less serious incidents such as a disabled vehicle, so the share of incident-related delays due to crashes should exceed the percentage of incidents that do not involve crashes). In 2010, there were about 6 million crashes in the United States, 93 percent of which can be attributed to human error (Maddox, 2012). AVs, if successful, should be able to prevent the vast majority of these crashes, in turn eliminating an appreciable share of all traffic delays.

Summary of effects on traffic congestion. Successful adoption of AVs, in short, could affect traffic congestion in several ways, as summarized in Table 2.2.

Based on the significant percentage of traffic congestion caused by crashes that AVs could help eliminate and the major improvements in throughput capacity they could enable, there is reason for optimism that the combined effects of these factors will be an overall reduction

Table 2.2
Summary of Autonomous Vehicle Technology on Traffic Congestion

Factor	Increase Traffic Congestion	Uncertain Effect	Decrease Traffic Congestion
Reduced travel costs	X		
Emergence of driverless taxi service		X	
Increase in road throughput capacity from more efficient vehicle operation			X
Reduced vehicle crashes			X

in traffic congestion, though this is far from certain. If such benefits do result, they will accrue not just to AV purchasers but also to the general motoring public, in the form of reduced negative congestion externalities created by automobile use.

Potential Effects on the Costs of Traffic Congestion

In contrast to remaining uncertainty regarding the effects of AVs on traffic congestion, the technology appears almost certain to offer major benefits in terms of reducing the *costs* associated with traffic congestion, particularly with respect to Level 3 and 4 automation.

Congested traffic imposes a range of social costs—including wasted time, excess fuel consumption, increased emission of local air pollutants and greenhouse gases, driver stress, diminished quality of life, and reduced economic efficiency. While many of these costs are hard to quantify, it is clear that the total costs associated with congestion are substantial.

In its annual *Urban Mobility Report*, the Texas A&M Transportation Institute (TTI) produces the most commonly cited statistics for the annual costs of congestion in the United States each year. TTI's computations focus on just three components of cost stemming from congestion delays: the value of time for personal travel (estimated at $16 per hour), the value of additional driver time and other operating costs for large trucks (estimated at $88 per hour), and the cost of excess fuel consumption (based on prevailing prices for gasoline and diesel). Based on data for 498 urban areas across the country, the authors of the 2012 report estimated that traffic congestion in 2011 resulted in roughly 5.5 billion total hours of excess travel delay and roughly 2.9 billion gallons of excess fuel consumption, representing a total cost of about $121 billion (Schrank et al., 2012). About 23 percent of the costs were associated with trucking delays, with the remainder applying to passenger travel.

The majority of the costs computed by TTI relate to additional travel time, with a smaller share resulting from excess fuel consumption. Because AVs should reduce the opportunity cost of travel time by freeing a driver to engage in other productive or enjoyable activities while driving, AVs could have a major impact in reducing the overall costs of congestion, even if traffic congestion itself is not significantly ameliorated. Of course, these computations do not include other costs associated with congestion, such as reduced economic efficiency, where AVs could also have a positive impact.

Unlike many of the other potential benefits of this technology, these benefits are realized by the user of the AV. Indeed, they are likely to be the prime motivation for the purchase or lease of such vehicles.

Land Use

The emergence and broad adoption of AVs could have a profound, if paradoxical, impact on prevailing land-use patterns. The prototypical form of cities can be explained in part by bid rent theory, first developed by J. H. von Thünen (1826) and further generalized by William Alonso (1964). (Additional theories, such as Walter Christaller's [1933] central place theory, provide some insight into the polycentric form of larger metropolitan regions.) In essence, bid rent theory posits that land's value increases with proximity to the central city, given the advantages of closer access to firms and markets. As one moves farther from the central city, land values decline and transportation costs rise.

Urban form, then, to the extent that it is unimpeded by zoning or other forms of land-use regulations, should reflect the aggregate effects of countless firms and individuals making location decisions based on tradeoffs between land values and transportation costs. In practice, this has resulted in a pattern, still common in many cities today, of a dense center-city area surrounded by moderate-density suburbs and fringed by low-density exurban settlements. An individual household might thus opt for a smaller home closer to the central business district, or a much larger suburban or exurban home at the cost of enduring a longer commute.

While AVs would not alter the underlying nature of trading off land values with transportation costs, they could have a major effect on the computation of the latter. For a typical auto commuter, transportation costs include not only such factors as depreciation, maintenance, insurance, and fuel costs, but also the value of the commuter's time—more specifically, the opportunity cost of other activities the driver might engage in otherwise. With conventional vehicles, drivers must focus most of their attention on the act of driving, precluding other substantive uses of their time. With Level 3 and 4 automation, in contrast, drivers would be free to engage in a range of other activities as the vehicle guides itself to the intended location. An AV owner might be able, for example, to work for two hours in the car on the way to work, spend four hours in the office, then work another two hours in the car on the way home.

Given the ability to engage in other activities while driving (or, more accurately, riding in) an AV, the cost of transportation declines. In weighing the tradeoffs between land values and transportation costs, this should increase the willingness of households, and possibly some firms, to locate farther away from the urban core. Just as the rise of the automobile in the 20th century led to the emergence of suburbs and ultimately exurbs by reducing transportation costs relative to earlier modes of travel, the introduction of AVs could strengthen a trend toward even more dispersed and low-density land-use patterns surrounding metropolitan regions.

In contrast, and somewhat paradoxically, AV technology could also lead to greater density in core urban areas. Here the main issue relates to parking supply and demand. Driving remains the dominant mode of passenger travel in the United States, even in large cities with good transit options. Yet, as Shoup notes in his exhaustive examination of parking policy (2005), the typical automobile is parked for about 95 percent of its lifetime. A significant amount of space must therefore be dedicated to parking, which reduces the overall density of land use. As an extreme example, Shoup estimates that if the total supply of parking in the Los Angeles central business district—including on-street parking, surface lots, and parking structures—were spread out at ground level, parking would occupy about 81 percent of the district area. Repeating the same computation for the central business districts in 41 major cities from around the world, Shoup determined that the total area devoted to parking spaces was equivalent, on average, to about 31 percent of the district area.

The emergence of AVs could sharply reduce the amount of parking needed in core urban areas in at least two ways. First, after dropping off its passenger or passengers in a downtown location, an AV could pilot itself to a remote lot in a peripheral area, reducing the amount of parking needed in the densest urban areas where land values are highest. Second, as described earlier, AV technology might lead to a new model for urban mobility in the form of driverless taxis. Under such a system, AVs often would not need to park; rather, after completing one trip, they would simply travel to pick up the next passenger. Additionally, the convenience and low cost of such a system would likely induce many urban dwellers to forgo car ownership, or at least to reduce the number of cars owned. Thus, driverless taxis could reduce the number of parking spaces needed in residential buildings as well as at commercial centers. These effects could free up substantial amounts of space in urban areas. On the other hand, by making parking unnecessary, this transition could threaten a reliable source of municipal revenue.

In short, the emergence and adoption of AV technology could lead to denser urban cores, increasing the amount of land and building space dedicated to human occupancy or some use other than parked cars. At the same time, AVs could support even greater dispersion of low-density development along the outskirts of major metropolitan areas given the ability of owners to engage in other activities as vehicles pilot themselves. These effects on land use are likely to occur over the long term and require the development of Level 4 automation.

AV technology may have different effects on land use in the developing world. Countries with limited existing vehicle infrastructure could "leapfrog" to AV technology. Just as mobile phones allowed developing countries to skip the development of expensive landline infrastructure, AV technology might permit countries to skip some aspects of conventional travel infrastructure. Such advancement might lead to completely different models of mobility; e.g., pervasive carsharing with efficient vehicles and road networks tailored to AVs. Further research to better understand how AV technology could affect the developing world's transportation needs would be useful.

Energy and Emissions Implications of Autonomous Vehicles

The use of light-duty passenger vehicles in the United States contributes to nearly 20 percent of national GHG emissions (EPA, 2013a). It also accounts for approximately 60 percent of petroleum use (Davis, Diegel, and Boundy, 2013), and is a major contributor to conventional air pollution such as smog and ground-level ozone. As is the case for safety, congestion, and land use, the transition to AVs has the potential to substantially affect the energy use, GHG emissions, and conventional air pollution impacts from the transportation sector, at least in the long term. Whether AVs improve or worsen energy use and environmental outcomes will depend on three factors:

- the fuel efficiency of AVs
- the carbon-intensity and life-cycle emissions profile of the fuel used to power AVs
- the total change in VMT resulting from use of AVs.

We will discuss the potential magnitude and direction of change that AVs could have on these three factors. Policymakers and other stakeholders can use this information to understand how near-term policies can affect the future energy and environmental outcomes from AVs.

Fuel Economy

AV technology can play a substantial role in improving fuel economy. Despite being heavier, advances in engine efficiency and vehicle design have increased fuel economy compared with the vehicles of the 1970s and 1980s, as shown in Figure 2.5. In 2012, the average fuel economy of cars was 27.3 mpg, while the fuel economy of trucks was 19.4 mpg (EPA, 2013b). CAFE standards were recently updated, and will require increased fuel economy from new vehicles to reach an average of 54.5 mpg in model year 2025. Advances in technology will enable fuel economy of conventional vehicles to continue to increase beyond that year. The NRC estimated the potential fuel economy improvements to conventional vehicles between now and 2050 to be 130 to 250 percent

Figure 2.5
Average Fuel Economy of U.S. Cars and Light Trucks, 1975–2012

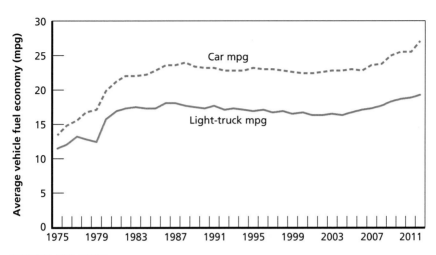

SOURCE: EPA, 2013b.
RAND *RR443-2.5*

(up to 87 and 110 mpg) for cars and 140 to 220 percent (up to 61 to 77 mpg) for light trucks (NRC, 2013a; 2011). The improvements stem from engine improvements as well as reductions in vehicle weight, drag, rolling resistance, and accessory loads. Conventional hybrid vehicles, already more efficient than traditional engines, would also see fuel economy improvements in these ranges, enabling up to 145 mpg.

Fuel economy improvements enabled by Level 1, 2, and 3 technology would first be realized through the automated and optimized driving, often referred to as "eco-driving." Examples are cruise control, smooth and gradual acceleration and deceleration, and other optimum driving habits that would be enabled through greater automation. Eco-driving can improve fuel economy by 4 to 10 percent (NRC, 2013a).

Additionally, since connected AVs can optimize traffic throughput and reduce the distance needed for safety between vehicles, AVs can eventually increase travel lane capacity and reduce fuel wasted during congestion. Over the course of the simulated driving cycles it uses to evaluate fuel economy, the EPA assumes vehicles are stopped or decelerating for 43.2 percent of the 7.5-mile city driving cycle, 9.3

percent of the 17.8-mile highway driving cycle, and 27.9 percent of the 10.3-mile CAFE driving cycle (Davis, Diegel, and Boundy, 2013). Vehicles that communicate with one another could reduce the time they are stopped, improving both traffic and drive-cycle efficiencies. Further, a platoon of closely spaced AVs that stops or slows down less often thereby resembles a train, enabling lower peak speeds (improving fuel economy) but higher effective speeds (improving travel time) (Folsom, 2012).

While the NRC studies (2011, 2013a) did not explicitly model improvements to fuel economy from AVs, they did speculate that networked AVs enabling safer, smaller vehicles could enable fuel consumption reductions more than twice their estimates for conventional and hybrid vehicles—and that pod car AVs (much smaller and lighter vehicles carrying one or two passengers) might reduce fuel consumption by an order of magnitude as compared to today's vehicles. Folsom (2012) estimates that a networked pod car AV system could enable fuel economies as much as 500 to 1,000 mpg.[9] Using these estimates, we present ranges of potential fuel economy improvements for conventional cars, hybrid cars, and autonomous cars (omitting light trucks) in Figure 2.6.

How Light Can We Make Vehicles If There Are Almost No Accidents? To move a vehicle, power is required to overcome inertia, rolling resistance (or "the street pushing back") and aerodynamic drag (or "the air pushing back"). Because of these factors, more power is required when the vehicle is heavier, going faster or uphill, or has a large frontal area. While a transition to AVs cannot change the topography of the driving area, AV technology can enable lighter and more aerodynamic vehicle designs.

The weight of vehicles directly affects the amount of power, and hence fuel, required for travel. Light-duty passenger vehicles in the United States are classified as either cars (such as sedans and smaller vehicles) or light trucks (such as sport-utility vehicles and other larger vehicles). For model year 2012, U.S. cars averaged 3,482 pounds and light trucks averaged 4,779 pounds, as shown in Figure 2.7. While the original Ford Model T only weighed 1,200 pounds and got between 13

---

[9] Car2go is an international car-sharing service that uses small Smart Fortwo cars.

Figure 2.6
Range of Potential Fuel Economy Improvements for Conventional, Hybrid, and Autonomous Cars

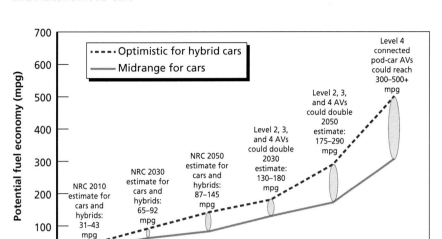

SOURCES: Analysis using data from NRC, 2013a; Folsom, 2012.
RAND RR443-2.6

and 21 mpg (Ford Motor Company, 2012), the lowest average weight for cars and trucks in more recent decades occurred in the early 1980s, when cars were 3,053 pounds and light trucks were 3,806 pounds, respectively (EPA, 2013b).

One of the most promising benefits of AVs is to dramatically reduce the number of accidents. As AVs are adopted and as technology progresses from Levels 0 through 4, AV technology could act as an effective substitute for some conventional, heavy, safety features. Thus, safety efforts are shifted from crashworthiness to accident avoidance. This has led some to propose AVs weighing 250 pounds that resemble pod-like motorcycles (Folsom, 2012).

However, the realization of these benefits will require AV consumers to have confidence that accidents with non-AVs are also avoided, which is likely to limit the types of substantial weight reduction to Level 3 or Level 4 automation and will depend upon nearly universal adoption of this technology so the risk from non-AVs is minimal. This

Figure 2.7
Average Weight of U.S. Cars and Light Trucks, 1975–2012

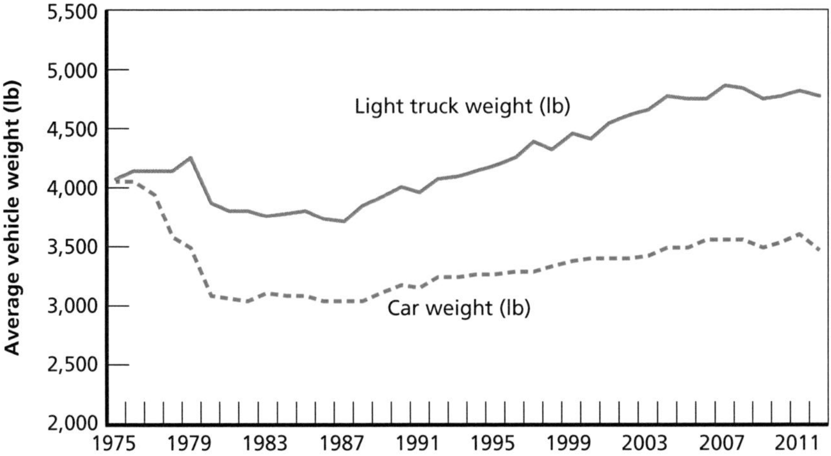

SOURCE: EPA, 2013b.

RAND *RR443-2.7*

weight reduction may also be slowed by retention of the current focus on crashworthiness by regulators and vehicle manufacturers. For this reason, we do not anticipate these benefits accruing for some time.

For conventional vehicles, reduction in weight of up to 20 percent is possible while maintaining vehicle size (NRC, 2013a). An engineering heuristic for vehicles is that a 10-percent reduction in weight results in a 6- to 7-percent reduction in fuel consumption (NHTSA/EPA/CARB, 2010). Weight reductions can be achieved primarily through substituting various lighter materials for traditional steel. These materials include high-strength steel (achieving the same steel strength with less material), aluminum, magnesium, plastics, and carbon-fiber composites (NRC, 2011). When vehicle weight is reduced, the engine and other components can be appropriately downsized, increasing fuel economy. Maintaining safety is a concern, as reducing weight in some vehicles has the potential to increase risk of fatalities in vehicle-to-vehicle collisions.

NHTSA and the EPA recently considered the effect of weight reductions on overall fatality risk. They concluded that weight reduction in small cars while holding vehicle size constant would increase societal fatality risk, but that weight reduction in larger light trucks and minivans would decrease or not affect societal fatality risk (NHTSA, 2012a). Since they expected that weight reductions employed to meet future fuel economy standards would occur on the heavier sport-utility vehicles and minivans, overall societal fatality risk would not be increased. While their review does not examine AVs, we can extrapolate that ultralight AVs operating in an environment alongside much heavier conventional vehicles without connectivity would likely increase societal fatality risk.

For any new technology there will be enthusiasts and first adopters, and the characteristics and benefits of AVs could be very attractive to many consumers and outweigh their perceived risks. After all, there are more than 8.2 million registered motorcycles in the United States (BTS, 2012a), and the design and safety features of AVs are highly likely to reduce fatality risk compared to motorcycles, even if they are much lighter than conventional vehicles. So weight reduction, and hence enhanced fuel economy, via AVs is likely to be realized in stages. The increased accident avoidance benefits of adoption and diffusion of vehicle automation Levels 1, 2, and 3 will help enable the vehicle weight reductions currently projected. These are substantial, projected as reductions of 20 to 25 percent by 2030 and of 32 to 50 percent by 2050 (NRC, 2013a). The successful deployment of Level 4 automation could then enable additional incremental weight reductions for conventionally designed vehicles. Level 4 technology might also permit radical redesigns of vehicles toward ultralight, aerodynamic pods. These lighter vehicles might first be used as taxis or car-sharing services in the urban core, eventually migrating to commuter and intercity use.

Autonomous Vehicles Might Enable Alternative Fuels

Petroleum products power more than 92 percent of U.S. transportation (Davis, Diegel, and Boundy, 2012). Unfortunately, their use creates significant negative externalities—conventional air pollution, GHG emissions, effects of relying on large amounts of imported petroleum, and others (see, for example, NRC, 2010; Michalek et al., 2011). Therefore, the diversification of transportation fuels and transition to alternative fuels and vehicles is a major U.S. research and policy objective (NRC, 2013a; 2013b). AV technology can enable and accelerate specific competitive aspects of alternative vehicles and fuels.

Conventional refined petroleum has considerable advantages as a transportation fuel. In about five minutes, one can fill up a car's tank with ten gallons of gasoline that contains about 360 kilowatt-hours (kWh) of energy. While the car's weight is increased by about 62 pounds, one can travel for about 300 miles in a 30-mpg vehicle (Shiau et al., 2009). As the gasoline is combusted during driving, the extra weight is gradually reduced. However, the efficiency of transforming that gasoline into driving power is only about 37 percent—a lot of that energy is lost as heat. An electric drivetrain has much fewer losses, and can exceed efficiencies of 90 percent (NRC, 2013a). The all-electric Nissan Leaf requires about 0.29 kWh per mile—equivalent to 115 mpg, or 0.009 gallons per mile (gpm)—while the conventional hybrid Toyota Prius requires 0.02 gpm, or gets 50 mpg (DOE/EPA, 2013). This is the primary reason it is nearly always cheaper to drive a mile using electricity as a fuel rather than gasoline (DOE, 2013). But storing electricity on a vehicle in a battery is both heavy and expensive. The battery that powers the Nissan Leaf holds about 24 kWh, weighs about 600 pounds, has a range of about 84 miles (Levin, 2013), takes four to seven hours or more to recharge (DOE/EPA, 2013), and, even under optimistic costs of $450/kWh (NRC, 2013a), would cost more than $10,000.

AV technologies can help enable a transition to electric and other alternative fuel vehicles. If automation Levels 2, 3, and 4 enabled the expected weight reductions, AVs fully or partially powered by electricity would be able to travel the same range using batteries that are smaller, and thus cheaper. The improved drive cycles and congestion management from Level 2, 3, and 4 AVs would also allow for smaller batteries. This would reduce the overall cost for consumers, and hasten the adoption of conventionally sized electrified vehicles. Smaller batteries would also reduce life-cycle environmental impacts from producing electric vehicle batteries, as well as reduce their environmental impacts at the end of their useful life (Hawkins, Gausen, and Strømman, 2012; Michalek et al., 2011; Samaras and Meisterling, 2008).

Level 4 vehicles, which are fully autonomous, are a potentially disruptive technology for the transition away from petroleum-powered passenger transportation. First, these AVs could make it easier for electrified vehicles to charge more often, which would minimize battery size and cost and maximize environmental benefits (Shiau et al., 2009). A Level 4 personal AV could drop its owners at a destination, then proceed to the nearest available charging station. These stations could initially be staffed akin to full-service gasoline stations to connect charging equipment, but eventually might require no human interaction, instead utilizing inductive wireless charging technology, currently being researched by the U.S. Department of Energy and others (NRC, 2013b). With vehicle-to-infrastructure (V2I) communication, wireless charging infrastructure could start out as fixed charging stations at parking places, then potentially advance toward in-roadway sections at traffic lights or other areas.

V2I communication could also allow for two-way charging through vehicle-to-grid interactions between electrified AVs and the electricity grid, at either wired or wireless connections. Two-way charging is a potential source of revenue, energy storage, and grid stabilization for a future grid with substantial renewables with variable production (Kempton and Tomić, 2005a; Kempton and Tomić, 2005b).

If Level 4 automation enables ultralight, pod-like AVs, these would require far smaller batteries to travel the same distance as a conventionally sized vehicle. Folsom (2012) pointed out that an experimental electric pod car has achieved 2,200 mpg equivalent at freeway speed, and that electric motorcycles have far greater range with a given battery capacity than electric vehicles. Level 4 automation also allows for vehicles specifically tailored to given tasks, which would also minimize energy and emissions. Taxi or car-sharing services could dispatch vehicles for any number of people (including just one), instead of the standard four- or five-seat sedan (Burns, 2013; Burns, Jordan, and Scarborough, 2013). Electric vehicles charged by low-carbon electricity have the potential to dramatically lower transportation GHG emissions, oil use, and conventional air pollutants (Samaras and Meisterling, 2008; Michalek et al., 2011). Level 2, 3, and 4 AVs can hasten this transition, with Level 4 AVs also enabling radical redesigns of both electric vehicles and the way consumers use them.

In addition to advancing electric vehicles, a lighter, more efficient car that drives itself to refueling areas could also enable other types of alternative powertrains, such as fuel cell vehicles. These cars use hydrogen as a fuel and have no tailpipe emissions during travel. But, unlike electric vehicles that can use the electricity grid as a nationwide refueling infrastructure, fuel cell vehicles would require construction of new hydrogen refueling infrastructure. The high cost of both producing the hydrogen and creating the infrastructure is one of the barriers for a viable fuel cell vehicle (NRC, 2013a). Level 4 AVs can travel to refueling stations without a driver, and hydrogen-refueling stations could be designed to autonomously fill up fuel cell vehicles. The refueling schedules and locations of connected Level 4 AVs could be optimized, and would allow fewer refueling stations to serve autonomous fuel cell vehicles than would be required if they were not autonomous.

The lightweighting permitted by AV technology could also increase a fuel cell vehicle's range and decrease its costs. Currently, a storage tank that holds 5 kilograms of hydrogen to enable a 300-mile plus range costs about $2,800, largely due to the carbon-fiber composite required to handle the high pressure of the compressed hydrogen (NRC, 2013b). A lighter fuel cell vehicle can travel farther on each kilogram of hydrogen fuel, so not as much hydrogen needs to be stored on the vehicle and vehicle costs are reduced. Level 2, 3, and 4 fuel cell AVs benefit from this and other efficiency gains of automation, but only driverless Level 4 fuel cell AVs reduce the amount of hydrogen refueling infrastructure needed.

How Will Travel Demand Affect Energy and Emissions?

As discussed above, AVs will have varying effects on the cost of mobility, vehicle throughput, congestion, and car ownership. All of these factors influence total VMT. Reduced travel costs from AVs will likely increase VMT, commonly referred to as the "rebound effect" and expressed as a percentage increase in VMT that results from a change in per-mile vehicle costs. NHTSA assumes a rebound rate of 10 percent for the base case and examines alternate cases of 5, 15, and 20 percent (NHTSA, 2012a). A 10-percent rebound effect means that if per-mile vehicle costs fall by 20 percent, VMT demand will rise by 2 percent.

In addition to existing drivers, the emergence of Level 4 AV taxis and car-sharing services may induce additional VMT demand from new sources. These include the elderly, the young, those without driver's licenses, and those who explicitly or implicitly value the time or multi-task opportunities afforded by driverless taxis at high rates. But if Level 4 driverless taxis are available, easy to use, and cheap, the incentive to own a vehicle is reduced, and declines in vehicle ownership rates would result. Table 2.3 outlines these and other potential impacts on total U.S. VMT.

The magnitude and direction of how AVs affect total VMT are key drivers of change in energy use and emissions from these vehicles.

However, even increases in total VMT can have neutral effects on energy and environmental impacts as long as vehicle efficiencies and/or GHG intensities of fuels are reduced. For example, in 2010, U.S. VMT per capita was 9,608 vehicle miles and VMT per vehicle in operation was 12,370 miles (Davis, Diegel, and Boundy, 2012). In a car that gets 31 mpg, one car would consume about 400 gallons of gasoline traveling 12,370 miles over the course of the year. If driving habits increased VMT and that vehicle is instead driven 20,000 miles per year, a 50-mpg car would be required to consume the same amount of gasoline annually.

The 12-month moving average of total U.S. VMT was 2.95 trillion in April 2012 (FHWA, 2013), of which about 10 percent was accounted for by medium and heavy trucks (BTS, 2012b). After peaking in 2008, total U.S. VMT has declined and leveled off, as shown in Figure 2.8.

Table 2.3
Potential Positive and Negative Effects on Total VMT

Influencing Factor	Increases VMT	Decreases VMT	Likely Automation Level
Rebound effect	X		2, 3, 4
Car-sharing and reduced vehicle ownership		X	2, 3, 4
Driverless taxis	X		4
Greater sprawl	X		2, 3, 4
Substitute for intracity or intercity public transportation	X		4

Figure 2.8
Annual Vehicle Miles Traveled in the United States

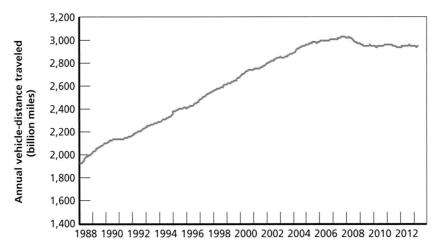

SOURCE: FHWA, 2013.
RAND RR443-2.8

The average fuel economy of new vehicles will increase, changing the fuel economy of the vehicle stock over time. The NRC estimates that traditional cars could get between 87 and 110 mpg by 2050 (NRC, 2013a). Fuel economy with Levels 2, 3, and 4 automation will be further enhanced, as discussed above. As a result of these efficiencies, as well as potential transitions to cleaner alternative fuels, the energy use and environmental impacts of the vehicle fleet will continue to be reduced. A key question will be if the fuel economy and emissions gains made from AV technologies Levels 2 through 4 will be large enough to outweigh any increases in VMT. As AVs are adopted, policymakers should understand and revisit this issue often, and make adjustments necessary to ensure energy and environmental goals are met.

Costs and Disadvantages

While there are reasons to think that AV technology may increase safety and efficiency, and reduce congestion and emissions per mile traveled, it may also lead to increased VMT with the associated negative externalities of increased fuel consumption, congestion, and suburban sprawl.

Parking is currently the source of considerable steady municipal income for many cities. By making proximate parking unnecessary, AVs may destroy this source of revenue. While parking may eventually be replaced by uses that generate tax revenue, the transition to AVs may substantially disrupt municipal finances.

Others have noted the potential social equity issues raised by AV technologies and argued that a focus on AVs distracts us from public transit (Arieff, 2013). Rather than improve transportation that can aid all citizens, focusing on AVs could merely perpetuate our individualistic car-centered society by starving public transit of riders. One of the current key attractions of public transit is that one can read or use a smartphone. When those activities can be done in a private car, fewer citizens may use mass transit. This, in turn, may reduce fare income and lead public transit authorities to either cut services or increase fare costs, which may create a vicious circle of declining transit ridership. AVs are also likely to be substantially more expensive than conventional cars, at least at first—exacerbating crash risk disparities between the rich and poor. However, these outcomes are not predetermined, and can be addressed through a variety of policy tools.

Jobs will also be lost. The act of driving is the source of many reasonably well-paid jobs. Recent immigrants often operate taxicabs or livery services, and municipal bus operations are the source of many union jobs. The commercial transportation sector employs thousands of professional drivers. Just as the invention of the automatic elevator led to the loss of many operator jobs, it is likely that AV technology will eventually lead to the loss of commercial transportation sector jobs at considerable human cost. Ultimately, the lost jobs might be replaced by others, perhaps related to the AV industry, but there may be considerable economic disruption.

The transition to AVs is likely to cause considerable economic disruption in other ways as well. American consumers spend approximately $157 billion in automobile insurance premiums every year (U.S. Census Bureau, 2012, p. 755). This supports not only insurance companies, but also doctors, lawyers, trauma centers, body shops, chiropractors and many others—an entire "crash economy." Automobile insurance companies are also important investors in federal, state, and municipal bonds. This entire sector of the economy may well be remade as crashes, and the wealth transfers they occasion, decline in frequency.

The eclipse of driving may also have cultural dimensions. Truck stops and institutions that cater to drivers may join the livery stable, commercial wharf, or airship dock as outmoded. The lures of the open road are very different if no driver is necessary. For example, the frenetic power of Jack Kerouac's *On the Road* depends, in part, on the epic cross-country drives that it chronicles. The book may lose some of its emotional power if driving becomes a rarity, pursued only by the eccentric or poor.

Conclusion

In this chapter, we compared AVs to conventional vehicles across a range of dimensions, including congestion, safety, and the environment. On the whole, we find that AVs offer considerable opportunity for improving social welfare, and could have significant benefits for both users and society at large, saving lives and costs in crash reduction at its early stages of development, and reducing congestion, environmental, and other externalities as technology and adoption levels increase. Fully automated vehicles could also increase transportation mobility and access to underserved populations, potentially at costs below those of existing paratransit services. On the other hand, some benefits of AV technology may lead to additional VMT, which may increase congestion and impose other external costs.

Since many AV benefits go to parties other than the purchasers of the technology, it is not clear whether consumers will be willing to purchase or lease this technology, an issue we return to in Chapter Eight. Policymakers considering efforts to internalize social benefits through subsidies or other mechanisms should conduct a benefit-cost analysis of AV technologies to inform these decisions. More research on the magnitudes of the potential costs and benefits and whether they go to the user of the AV or others would be useful.

CHAPTER THREE

Current State Law and Legislative Activity

Interest in driverless cars has led to a flurry of recent legislative activity. Four states and the District of Columbia have passed legislation authorizing the testing of AVs. Nevada took the lead in June 2011 with a law that outlined a broad framework for regulating AVs and directed the Nevada DMV (NDMV) to produce regulations (R084-11), which took effect March 1, 2012 (NDMV, 2012). Florida (Florida Statutes, 2012), California (California Vehicle Code, 2012), and Washington, D.C. (District of Columbia, 2013) followed Nevada, with legislation enacted in April 2012, September 2012, January 2013, and May 2013, respectively. Michigan passed a bill in December of 2013 that goes into effect on March 27, 2014.

It is not clear that legislation was necessary to permit testing or even operation of a driverless vehicle; Bryant Walker Smith has argued that existing law probably permits the use of driverless cars (Smith, 2012b). Nor are we aware of any documented problems with the testing or use of AVs that the legislation addresses. On the other hand, it begins the conversation between legislators, stakeholders, and regulators about how these vehicles and their operators should be regulated.

There are important similarities and differences in this raft of legislation. All of the enacted measures and implementing regulations similarly define AVs as vehicles with the capability to self-drive without being actively controlled or monitored by a human operator. This excludes vehicles enabled with active safety systems or driver assistance systems, including sideview (blind spot) assistance, crash avoidance, emergency braking, parking assistance, ACC, lane keeping assistance, lane departure warning, or traffic jam and queuing assistance, without the capability to self-navigate. The enacted legislation generally defines the operator as the person who engages the technology. A notable distinction in Nevada's regime is that it requires the driver of an AV to obtain a "certificate of compliance," either from the manufacturer of the vehicle or from a state-certified technology certification facility, if the driver wishes to operate the AV in nontesting mode. In this respect, Nevada's law anticipates the future commercialization of AVs.

Nevada's Certificate of Compliance

Section 16 of the Nevada regulation stipulates, "Before an AV may be offered for sale by a licensed vehicle dealer in this State, a certificate of compliance must be issued for the autonomous technology installed on the AV by: (a) The manufacturer of the AV; or (b) An autonomous technology certification facility that is licensed pursuant to section 19 of this regulation" (NDMV, 2012). It is unclear what additional cost this certification requirement will impose on end users. The regulation states, however, that "autonomous technology certification facilities," which are private entities that receive endorsement from the DMV, are required to pay a sum of $300 and a surety bond of $500,000 to operate. A Nevada driver who obtains a technology certification from the facility will receive a special endorsement on his or her state driver's license.

Nevada's compliance regulations impose several specific technical requirements for AVs. For example, certificates issued pursuant to the Nevada regulations must certify that, along with various provisions concerning the safety of the operation of the vehicle, the AV has

> a separate mechanism in addition to, and separate from, any other mechanism required by law, to capture and store the autonomous technology sensor data for at least 30 seconds before a collision occurs between the autonomous vehicle and another vehicle, object or natural person while the vehicle is operating in autonomous mode. The autonomous technology sensor data must be captured and stored in a read-only format by the mechanism so

that the data is retained until extracted from the mechanism by an external device capable of downloading and storing the data. Such data must be preserved for 3 years after the date of the collision. The provisions of this paragraph do not authorize or require the modification of any other mechanism to record data that is installed on the autonomous vehicle in compliance with federal law. (NDMV, 2012)

Since the text refers to "a separate mechanism in addition to, and separate from" any other, it appears that this new device would be in addition to the Event Data Recorder (EDR) required by NHTSA. The regulation does not address who will have access to these data, or whether they belong only to the AV owner.

Licensed dealers in Nevada can only sell AVs with certifications issued by the manufacturer or an authorized autonomous technology certification facility. The certification must also attest that the AV includes "a switch to engage and disengage the autonomous vehicle that is easily accessible to the operator of the autonomous vehicle and is not likely to distract the operator from focusing on the road while engaging or disengaging the autonomous vehicle," "a visual indicator inside the autonomous vehicle, which indicates when the autonomous vehicle is engaged in autonomous mode," and a "system to safely alert the operator of the autonomous vehicle if a technology failure is detected while the autonomous vehicle is engaged in autonomous mode," among other requirements. The California legislation requires a similar certification by a manufacturer of AVs.

Comparison of State Legislation

Florida, Nevada, and Washington, D.C., laws provide liability protection for original equipment manufacturers whose vehicles are converted to autonomous controls, while there is no explicit mention of such liability protection in the California measure. Other states with draft bills contain diverse treatments of liability issues. Colorado, for example, retains liability for damages with the driver who may or may not use autonomous "guidance technology," while other states, such as

Hawaii, absolve manufacturers of liability where a car has been retrofitted by a third party and operator (or driver) where there is no verifiable "recklessness" identified. South Carolina, like California, redefines "manufacturer" as whoever is responsible for installation of autonomous technology, either the original manufacturer or upfitter.

We now summarize some of the key characteristics of the AV laws and regulations that have been enacted to date.

Nevada (NRS 482.A and NAC 482.A)

- **Enacted:** June 2011, revised July 1, 2013.
- **Definition of AVs:** "Autonomous technology" means technology which is installed on a motor vehicle and which has the capability to drive the motor vehicle without the active control or monitoring of a human operator. The term does not include an active safety system or a system for driver assistance, including, without limitation, a system to provide electronic blind spot detection, crash avoidance, emergency braking, parking assistance, adaptive cruise control, lane keeping assistance, lane departure warning, or traffic jam and queuing assistance, unless any such system, alone or in combination with any other system, enables the vehicle on which the system is installed to be driven without the active control or monitoring of a human operator.
- **Intent:** Testing, individual ownership.
- **What must the AV have?** Vehicle must possess a certificate of compliance stating that the AV is capable of being operated in autonomous mode without the physical presence of the operator in the vehicle. Licensed dealers can only sell AVs with certifications issued by the manufacturer or an authorized technology certification facility.
- **Who can operate?** The regulation stipulates an endorsement on driver's license to operate.
- **Technology certification facility:** Creates a privately operated technology certification facility market. Applicants to operate technology certification facilities must demonstrate the necessary knowledge and expertise to certify the safety of AVs, pay a nonre-

fundable fee of $300, and provide a surety bond or deposit of cash in lieu of the bond in the amount of $500,000.

- **Liability:** Manufacturer not liable for damages if vehicle is converted by third party.
- **Requirements of DMV:** The DMV was directed to draft and adopt regulations by March 1, 2012.
- **Insurance for testing:** Applicants for testing must pay a nonrefundable fee of $100 along with a surety bond of $1 million for testing fewer than five AVs, $2 million for six to nine, or $3 million for ten or more.
- **Exceptions:** Restricts the testing of AVs to specified geographic areas.

Florida (Fla. Stat. Title XXIII, Ch. 319, S 145)

- **Enacted:** April 2012.
- **Definition of AVs:** "Autonomous technology" means technology installed on a motor vehicle that has the capability to drive the vehicle on which the technology is installed without the active control of or monitoring by a human operator (Florida Statutes, 2012). Excludes vehicles "enabled with active safety systems or driver assistance systems, including, without limitation, a system to provide electronic blind spot assistance, crash avoidance, emergency braking, parking assistance, adaptive cruise control, lane keep assistance, lane departure warning, or traffic jam and queuing assistant, unless any such system alone or in combination with other systems enables the vehicle on which the technology is installed to drive without the active control or monitoring by a human operator" (Florida House of Representatives, 2012).
- **Intent:** Testing, development, and operation.
- **What must the AV have?** Vehicles must meet federal standards and regulations for motor vehicles and comply with applicable traffic and motor vehicle laws of Florida; have safety mechanisms for engaging and disengaging the technology; have indicators inside the vehicle that show when the vehicle is in autonomous mode, a means of alerting the operator of a technology failure; and have a human operator present to monitor the vehicle's per-

formance and intervene, if necessary, unless the vehicle is being tested or demonstrated on a closed course.

- **Who can operate?** Vehicles may be operated by persons with a valid driver's license.
- **Liability:** The original manufacturer of a vehicle converted by a third party into an AV is not liable for injury due to an alleged vehicle defect caused by the conversion of the vehicle, or by equipment installed by the converter, unless the alleged defect was present in the vehicle as originally manufactured.
- **Requirements of DMV:** The DMV was required to prepare and submit a report relating to the safe operation of vehicles equipped with autonomous technology by February 12, 2014.
- **Insurance for testing:** Prior to the start of testing in the state, applicants must submit an instrument of insurance, surety bond, or proof of self-insurance acceptable to the department in the amount of $5 million.
- **Exceptions:** Federal regulations supersede this law when in conflict.

California (Cal. Veh. Code, Division 16.6)

- **Enacted:** September 2012.
- **Definition of AVs:** "'Autonomous technology' is defined as technology that has the capability to drive a vehicle without the active physical control or monitoring of a human operator" (California Vehicle Code, 2012). "Autonomous vehicle" means any "vehicle equipped with autonomous technology that has been integrated into that vehicle. Does not include a vehicle that is equipped with one or more collision avoidance systems, including, but not limited to, electronic blind spot assistance, automated emergency braking systems, park assist, adaptive cruise control, lane keep assist, lane departure warning, traffic jam and queuing assist, or other similar systems that enhance safety or provide driver assistance, but are not capable, collectively or singularly, of driving the vehicle without the active control or monitoring of a human operator."
- **Intent:** Testing and operation.

- **What must the AV have?** Vehicles must possess manufacturer certification of a mechanism to engage and disengage the autonomous technology; a visual indicator to indicate when the autonomous technology is engaged; a system to safely alert the operator if an autonomous technology failure is detected while the autonomous technology is engaged, and when an alert is given; and a driver in the driver's seat, monitoring the safe operation of the AV, who is capable of taking over immediate manual control.
- **Who can operate?** For testing, only employees, contractors, or other persons designated by the manufacturer of the autonomous technology with the proper class of license for the type of vehicle being operated.
- **Liability:** No mention of liability.
- **Requirements of DMV:** Directs the DMV to draft and adopt regulations by January 2015.
- **Insurance for testing:** Prior to the start of testing in this state, the manufacturer performing the testing must obtain an instrument of insurance, surety bond, or proof of self-insurance in the amount of $5 million.
- **Exceptions:** Does not make inoperative other safety standards and performance requirements required by state and federal law.

Washington, D.C. (L19-0278)
- **Enacted:** January 2013.
- **Definition of AVs:** "A vehicle capable of navigating District roadways and interpreting traffic control devices without a driver actively operating any of the vehicle's control systems." "Excludes a motor vehicle enabled with active safety systems or driver assistance systems, including a system to provide electronic blind spot assistance, crash avoidance, emergency braking, parking assistance, adaptive cruise control, lane keep assistance, lane departure warning, or traffic jam and queuing assistance, unless a system alone or in combination with other systems enables the vehicle on which the technology is installed to drive without active control or monitoring by a human operator" (District of Columbia, 2013).

- **Intent:** Testing and operation.
- **What must the AV have?** Vehicle must have a manual override feature that allows a driver to assume control of the AV at any time, and must be capable of operating in compliance with the District's applicable traffic and motor vehicle laws and traffic control devices.
- **Liability:** The original manufacturer of a vehicle converted by a third party into an AV is not liable in any action resulting from a vehicle defect caused by the conversion of the vehicle, or by equipment installed by the converter, unless the alleged defect was present in the vehicle as originally manufactured (District of Columbia, 2013, §4). The conversion of vehicles into AVs is limited to model years 2009 and later, or vehicles built within four years of conversion, whichever vehicle is newer.

Ongoing Legislation in Other States

In addition to the four jurisdictions that already have effective laws defining and regulating AVs, there is considerable legislative activity on this issue in many other states. These are summarized below:

Arizona (HB 2167)
- **Introduced:** January 2013.
- **Status:** Introduced.
- **Key features:** Defines AVs and autonomous technology (excludes individual driver assist systems) (Arizona State Legislature, 2013), removes liability from vehicle manufacturer when autonomous technology is fitted by third party, cedes priority to federal laws where there is a conflict (Arizona State Legislature, 2013 §1-B), and requires a report from the Arizona Department of Technology by April 2015 recommending additional legislation (Arizona State Legislature, 2013, §2).

Colorado (SB 13-016)
- **Introduced:** January 2013.

- **Status:** Indefinitely postponed.
- **Key Features:** Defines "drive" and redefines "driver" in the vehicle code to include minors under the age of 21 or anyone who may use "guidance systems to drive" (Colorado General Assembly, 2013) but retains that "[t]he driver is responsible for any damage caused by a motor vehicle being driven by means of a guidance system to the same degree as if the driver were manually driving the vehicle," and that drivers must be duly licensed (Colorado General Assembly, 2013, §4), eliminates following-distance restrictions for AVs (Colorado General Assembly, 2013, §5), and directs the department of revenue and the state patrol to submit a joint report by August 30, 2018 (Colorado General Assembly, 2013, §4).

Hawaii (HB 1461)

- **Introduced:** January 2013.
- **Status:** Committee.
- **Key Features:** Defines AVs and technology (excludes individual driver assist systems) (Hawaii State Legislature, 2013); absolves manufacturer (defined as original manufacturer or retrofitter) of liability where car is retrofitted by a third party, and operator where there is no verifiable "recklessness" identified (Hawaii State Legislature, 2013, §286-D); requires "the director" (presumably of the DMV) to adopt rules for AV operation by January 2, 2015 (Hawaii State Legislature, 2013, §286-E); also requires an annual report from the director that includes an evaluation of feasibility and safety of AVs and progress of testing and applications (Hawaii State Legislature, 2013, §286-F).

Massachusetts (HB 3369)

- **Introduced:** January 2013.
- **Status:** Committee.
- **Key Features:** Defines AVs and autonomous technology (excludes individual driver assist systems); removes liability from vehicle manufacturer when autonomous technology is fitted by a third party; requires a report from the division of highway safety by February 12, 2015, recommending additional legislation; and

cedes priority federal laws where there is a conflict (Massachusetts General Court of the Commonwealth, 2013).

Michigan (SB 0169)

- **Introduced:** February 2013.
- **Status:** Passed, effective date, March 27, 2014.
- **Key Features:** Defines "automated technology," "automated vehicle," "automated mode," and "upfitter"; grants civil liability immunity to manufacturers of automated technology for damages that arise out of any modification made by another person to a motor vehicle or an automated motor vehicle; and directs state DOT and Secretary of State to submit a report by February 1, 2016, to recommend further legislative and regulatory action (Michigan Legislature, 2013).

New Hampshire (HB 444)

- **Introduced:** January 2013.
- **Status:** Inexpedient to legislate.
- **Key Features:** Establishes a committee of legislators "to study the use of autonomous vehicles in New Hampshire" and instructs the committee to deliver a report by November 1, 2013 (New Hampshire General Court, 2013).

New Jersey (A2757)

- **Introduced:** May 2012.
- **Status:** Committee.
- **Key Features:** Defines "autonomous vehicle," "artificial intelligence," and "sensors" and directs state Motor Vehicle Commission to adopt rules for driver's license endorsements and for operation, including insurance, safety standards, and testing (New Jersey Legislature, 2012).

New York (S4912)

- **Introduced:** May 2013.
- **Status:** Committee.

- **Key Features:** Defines "autonomous technology" and "autonomous vehicles" (New York State Senate, 2013); defines conditions for testing; absolves original manufacturer, distributor, or dealer of liability for defect due to equipment installed upon conversion (New York State Senate, 2013, §9-303); and directs the commissioner of motor vehicles to study operation and testing, and report by February 12, 2015 (New York State Senate, 2013, §7).

Oklahoma (HB 3007)
- **Introduced:** January 2012.
- **Status:** Committee.
- **Key Features:** Defines "autonomous vehicle," "artificial intelligence," and "sensors," and directs state Department of Public Safety to adopt rules for license endorsement and for operation, including insurance, safety standards, and testing of AVs (Oklahoma Legislature, 2012).

Oregon (HB 2428)
- **Introduced:** January 2013.
- **Status:** Committee.
- **Key Features:** Defines "autonomous system," "autonomous vehicle," and "manufacturer" (Oregon State Legislature, 2013); establishes application procedure and conditions for testing of AVs (Oregon State Legislature, 2013, §3); directs the DMV to adopt rules for testing; establishes requirements (similar to California's) for data recording and disclosure (Oregon State Legislature, 2013, §6); absolves original manufacturer of liability for a vehicle on which a third party has installed an autonomous system (Oregon State Legislature, 2013, §7).

South Carolina (HB 4015)
- **Introduced:** April 2013.
- **Status:** Committee.
- **Key Features:** Defines "autonomous technology," "autonomous vehicle," "operator," and "manufacturer" (South Carolina General Assembly, 2013); defines conditions for testing (South Caro-

lina General Assembly, 2013, §56-12-10-70); directs the DMV to adopt regulation by January 1, 2015 (South Carolina General Assembly, 2013, §56-12-80). Manufacturer is defined as whoever installs autonomous technology on vehicle (original manufacturer or upfitter).

Texas (HB 2932)

- **Introduced:** March 2013.
- **Status:** Committee.
- **Key Features:** Defines "autonomous motor vehicle," "autonomous technology," and "operator"; requires operator to be licensed; and directs the "department" to "adopt rules authorizing" and regulating "the operation of autonomous motor vehicles" (Texas Legislature, 2013).

Washington (HB 1649)

- **Introduced:** January 2013.
- **Status:** Reintroduced.
- **Key Features:** Defines "autonomous technology" (Washington State Legislature, 2013), establishes requirements for testing, establishes general requirements for vehicles controlled by autonomous technology (Washington State Legislature, 2013, §§3,4,5), and directs the department of licensing to "review statutes and rules regarding AVs and report on June 30, 2026" (Washington State Legislature, 2013, §6).

Wisconsin (SB 80)

- **Introduced:** March 2013.
- **Status:** Conducted fiscal estimates.
- **Key Features:** Defines "autonomous vehicle," "autonomous technology," and "autonomous mode" (Wisconsin Legislature, 2013); defines "manufacturer" (Wisconsin Legislature, 2013, §3); specifies certain conditions for the testing and operation of such vehicles (including the presence of a human operator) (Wisconsin Legislature, 2013, §4).

Stakeholder Interviews

A number of stakeholders from different organizations expressed concern during interviews that a plethora of conflicting state laws could hamper deployment of AVs. Executives of an original equipment manufacturer (OEM) explained the difficulties of manufacturing AVs for the U.S. market if they have to meet different sets of standards to sell vehicles in different states, noting that manufacturers need a framework that works in all 50 states. State law variation might also hinder purchasers of AVs, if they are required to obtain specific operational endorsements that vary among states. It is also unclear whether these laws are really necessary at this point, given the lack of any vehicles for sale. One stakeholder even suggested that legislators were more interested in getting in the news than in solving any actual problems by passing legislation.

Conclusion

In this chapter, we briefly reviewed current laws and regulations and the considerable ongoing legislative activity in this area.[1] Inconsistent state laws might increase costs and hinder the use of this technology in a way that harms social welfare for little apparent gain. We are unaware of any reported accidents or harm from AV technology or testing at this point. We would suggest that state lawmakers proceed cautiously in this area and adopt legislative solutions only in response to clearly identified problems. Further efforts to develop a model statute to promote uniformity in requirements may be useful.[2]

---

[1] Bryant Walker Smith has argued that AVs are most likely legal under existing laws (Smith, 2012a).

[2] See Smith (2012a) for an example of such a model statute.

CHAPTER FOUR

Brief History and Current State of Autonomous Vehicles

In this chapter, we review the history of AV technology and the technology's status as of July 2013. Our goal is to provide a nontechnical summary of the technology and its limitations for an interested policy audience. The current state of technology in particular is relevant for several near-term policy decisions:

- Will states need to regulate AV models that may each have different operating limitations—and, if so, how?
- What kinds of safety testing and verification will be required before the first AV is commercially available?
- What near-term actions can state and federal transportation agencies take to increase the safety of AVs, given their financial constraints and the uncertainty in the development of AVs?

A Brief History

Visions of AVs and automated highways in the mid–20th century remained largely in the eye of futurists and science fiction enthusiasts. In 1958, for example, Disney aired a program titled "Magic Highway USA" that imagined a future with, among other technologies, AVs guided by colored highway lanes and operated with addresses coded on punch cards. It was not until the mid-1980s that the underlying computing and other technologies needed to realize (and revise) these visions truly became available. The advances made in the last 25 years can be understood in terms of three successive waves of developmental gains.

Phase 1: Foundational Research

From approximately 1980 to 2003, university research centers, sometimes in partnership with transportation agencies and automotive companies, undertook basic studies of autonomous transportation. Two main technology concepts emerged from this work.

As one thrust, researchers pursued the development of automated highway systems, in which vehicles depend significantly on the highway infrastructure to guide them. One of the first major demonstrations of such a system took place in 1997, over a 7.6-mile stretch of California's I-15 highway near San Diego. Led by the California Partners for Advanced Transit and Highways (PATH) program, the "DEMO 97" program demonstrated the platooning of eight AVs guided by magnets embedded in the highway and coordinated with vehicle-to-vehicle (V2V) communication (Ioannou, 1998).

A second research thrust was to develop both semi-autonomous and autonomous vehicles that depended little, if at all, on highway infrastructure. In the early 1980s, a team led by Ernst Dickmanns at Bundeswehr University Munich in Germany developed a vision-guided vehicle that navigated at speeds of 100 kilometers per hour without traffic (Lantos and Mâarton, 2011). Carnegie Mellon University's NavLab developed a series of vehicles, named NavLab 1 through NavLab 11, from the mid-1980s to the early 2000s. In July 1995, NavLab 5 drove across the country in a "No Hands Across America" tour, in which the vehicle steered autonomously 98 percent of the time while human operators controlled the throttle and brakes. Other similar efforts around the world sought to develop and advance initial AV and highway concepts.

Phase 2: Grand Challenges

From 2003 to 2007, the U.S. Defense Advanced Research Projects Agency (DARPA) held three "Grand Challenges" that markedly accelerated advancements in AV technology and reignited the public's imagination. The first two Grand Challenges charged research teams with developing vehicles that were fully autonomous for competition in a 150-mile off-road race for $1 million and $2 million prizes, respectively. No vehicle completed the 2004 Grand Challenge—the best competitor completed less than eight miles of the course ("Desert Race Too Tough for Robots," 2004). However, five teams successfully completed the 2005 Grand Challenge course, held a mere 18 months later. The fastest team completed the course in just under seven hours, with the next three fastest vehicles finishing within the next 35 minutes (DARPA, undated).

In 2007, DARPA held its third and final AV challenge, dubbed the "Urban Challenge." As the name suggests, vehicles raced through a 60-mile urban course, obeying traffic laws and navigating alongside other autonomous and human-driven vehicles. Six teams finished the course, and three completed the race within a time of 4.5 hours, including time penalties for violating traffic and safety rules. This Grand Challenge spearheaded advancements in sensor systems and computing algorithms to detect and react to the behavior of other vehicles, to navigate marked roads, and to obey traffic rules and signals.

Phase 3: Commercial Development

The DARPA Challenges solidified partnerships between auto manufacturers and the education sector, and it mobilized a number of endeavors in the automotive sector to advance AVs. These include the Autonomous Driving Collaborative Research Lab, a partnership between GM and Carnegie Mellon University (Carnegie Mellon University, undated) and a partnership between Volkswagen and Stanford University (Stanford University, undated).

Google's Driverless Car initiative has brought autonomous cars from the university laboratory into commercial research. The program began shortly after the DARPA Urban Challenge and drew upon the talents of engineers and researchers from several teams that participated in that competition. In the years since, Google has developed and tested a fleet of cars and initiated campaigns to demonstrate the applications of the technology through, for example, videos highlighting mobility offered to the blind (Google, 2012). Google is not alone. In 2013, Audi and Toyota both unveiled their AV visions and research programs at the International Consumer Electronics Show, an annual event held every January in Las Vegas (Hsu, 2013).

State of Autonomous Vehicle Technology

As of March 2013, Google alone had logged more than 500,000 miles of autonomous driving on public roads without incurring a crash attributable to the technology.[1] Numerous technological breakthroughs have made these achievements possible, including advanced sensors to gather information about the world, increasingly sophisticated algorithms to process sensor data and control the vehicle, and more computational power to run them in real time.

AVs like Google's that drive on public roads are currently operated by specially trained human operators who take control of the vehicle in dangerous or unexpected conditions, including roadwork, inclement weather, and near crashes. Ultrareliability seems a prerequisite for vehicles that are fully autonomous—i.e., vehicles in which the driver plays no role in the driving task, and for driverless cars, which may have no driver in the vehicle at all. Such reliability is extremely difficult to achieve in a dynamic and complex environment in which many factors fall beyond the control of vehicle designers or operators.[2] Yet, such capabilities may be necessary if AVs are to deliver on their potential of being extremely safe, light, and efficient vehicles; of offering mobility to those who lack it; of creating new models of vehicle ownership and new land-use patterns; and of reshaping commerce. In this section, we briefly discuss current AV technology, its limitations, and possible ways forward.

Making Sense of the World

In the most general terms, AVs employ a "sense-plan-act" design that is the foundation of many robotic systems.[3] A suite of sensors on the vehicle gathers raw data about the outside world and the vehicle's relation to its environment. Software algorithms interpret the sensor data—e.g., lane markings from images of the road, behavior of other vehicles from

---

[1]   In 2011, a Google AV was involved in a minor crash, but a human driver was operating it at the time (Yarrow, 2011).

[2]   By way of contrast, commercial aircraft operate in a much simpler environment and, among other things, make use of air traffic control for guidance and coordination with other aircraft.

[3]   See, generally, Siciliano and Khatib (2008).

radar data. They use these data to make plans about the vehicle's own actions—its overall trajectory down the road and immediate decisions such as accelerating and changing directions. These plans are converted into actionable commands to the vehicle's control system; i.e., steering, throttle, brakes. Many "sense-plan-act" loops may run in parallel on an AV. One loop may run at extremely high frequency to initiate rapid emergency braking, while another runs less frequently to plan and execute complex behaviors such as changing lanes. In some cases, the planning component of the loop is extremely short and resembles a sense-act cycle instead of a sense-plan-act cycle. For instance, a vehicle may gather data about obstacles immediately in front of it at very high frequency and initiate emergency braking if any obstacle is detected within a short distance. In this case, the sensor data may directly trigger a vehicle action.

With perfect perception (a combination of sensor data gathering and interpretation of those data), AVs could plan and act perfectly, achieving ultrareliability. Vehicles never tire; their planning algorithms can choose provably optimal behaviors; and their execution can be fast and flawless.[4] For example, if a deer were to leap into the path of a human-driven vehicle, the driver may make mistakes in choosing whether to swerve, brake, or take another course of action. The driver may also make mistakes in executing the action; e.g., oversteering a swerve. AVs need never make these mistakes. Computer algorithms can rapidly evaluate, compare, select, and execute the best action from among a number of maneuvers, taking into account the vehicle's speed, the animal's trajectory, the position and behavior of other vehicles, and the utility of various outcomes.

---

[4] Not all robotic behaviors are as well developed as vehicle navigation, which has been studied for decades. Other actions are difficult for robots to perform, such as folding an item of clothing or separating the filling from an Oreo cookie. Both have received significant research attention. While these manipulation tasks include challenging perception problems, they additionally require planning with many more degrees of freedom and with difficult constraints on the robot. As such, they cannot rely on traditional planning algorithms, which often involve two or three dimensions (Cusumano-Towner et al., 2011; Hornyak, 2013).

One of the more difficult challenges for AVs is making sense of the complex and dynamic driving environment—e.g., perceiving the deer. The driving environment includes many elements:

- other vehicles on the road, each of which operates dynamically and independently
- other road users or on-road obstacles, such as pedestrians, cyclists, wildlife, and debris
- weather conditions, from sunny days to severe storms
- infrastructure conditions, including construction, rough road surfaces, poorly marked roads, and detours
- traffic events, such as congestion or crashes.

It is in making sense of the world that humans often outperform robots. Human eyes are sophisticated and provide nearly all of the sensory data we use to drive. We are also adept at interpreting what we see. Although our eyes are passive sensors, only receiving information from reflected light, we can judge distances; recognize shapes and classify objects such as cars, cycles, and pedestrians; and see in a tremendous range of conditions. Of course, we are far from perfect. Our sight and our cognition of visual information vary and can be dangerously limited in several situations: adverse ambient conditions such as darkness, rain, and fog; when we are tired or distracted; and when we are impaired through the use of drugs or alcohol (Olson, Dewar, and Ferber, 2010).

Camera-based systems, i.e., computer vision systems, are the analogy to human eyes and visual cognition. They can "see" very long distances and provide rich information about everything in their field of view. Cameras are also inexpensive, making them important components for cost-effective autonomy. However, they have two important limitations. First, the underlying algorithms are not nearly as sophisticated as humans at interpreting visual data. The Solutions in Perception Challenge is an annual competition that embodies this difference, challenging engineering teams to develop computer vision and other sensor algorithms that can detect, recognize, and locate objects. In the 2011 competition, for example, the objects included a number of items that would be found on supermarket shelves. None of the competing teams reached the goal of 80 percent accuracy (Markoff, 2011).

A second limitation is that, like human eyes, camera systems are better able to gather data in some ambient conditions (e.g., clear sunny days) than others (e.g., fog or rainstorms). Changes in ambient conditions also pose challenges, as camera systems calibrated to certain conditions may have difficulty interpreting data in others. This problem of autonomous camera calibration is also a fundamental robotics research problem (Furukawa and Ponce, 2009).

Of course, AVs have a critical advantage over humans: they can draw upon a much wider array of sensor technologies than cameras alone.[5] While many major advances have been made in the last decade, interpretation of visual data (and sensor data more generally) remains a fundamental research problem in the field of computer vision. We can expect advances in both sensor technology and perception algorithms, but matching human perception under best conditions is a long-term research challenge. Here, we review a few of the most widely used sensors, besides cameras, for driver assistance and AVs.

Sensor Systems

Light detection and ranging, or *lidar*, systems feature prominently in robotic systems, including AVs. Lidar systems determine distances to obstacles by using laser range finders, which emit light beams and calculate the time-of-flight until a reflection is returned by objects in the environment. Many sophisticated lidars couple multiple laser range finders with rapidly rotating mirrors to generate three-dimensional point clouds of the environment. Developed during the DARPA Grand Challenges and used by teams in the Urban Challenge and by Google, the Velodyne HDL-64E lidar uses 64 lasers that provide 1.3 million data points per second and offer a 360-degree field of view. Lidars are typically useful over a shorter range than other sensors—the Velodyne provides data up to 120 meters away, depending on the reflectivity of the object. Lidar systems' two key limitations are

---

[5]   This is the aim of increasingly prevalent driver assistance systems that provide the driver with data and warnings about the driving environment, e.g., rear-facing cameras and radar sensors that warn the driver when an obstacle is in the vehicle's path.

range (less useful at long ranges) and reflectivity (poor reflection off of certain kinds of materials). The Velodyne's specifications state that it detects black asphalt, which has low reflectivity, to a range of just 50m (Velodyne, 2010). The costs of lidar systems range widely but are expected to decline in the near future. Google originally paid approximately $70,000 for the lidar system on a single vehicle, including a Velodyne lidar. However, the German lidar manufacturer Ibeo has stated it will provide lidar systems for $250 per vehicle in 2014 (Priddle and Woodyard, 2012).

Radio detection and ranging, more commonly known as *radar*, is another key sensor for AVs. Like lidar, radar systems use signals' time of flight to determine the range to objects in the environment. Unlike lidar, radar uses radio waves, which give radar systems different capabilities and limitations. The reflectivity limitations of radar are typically even more severe than those of lidar: It works well on metallic objects, such as vehicles, but nonmetallic objects, such as pedestrians, are essentially invisible to a radar sensor. Pedestrian detection using radar has become a key area of research in automotive radar, given increasing use in driver assistance systems (Panasonic, 2012). Radar systems used for ACC can currently add approximately $1,000 to the price of vehicles, though manufacturers are continuing efforts to reduce sensor cost (Stevenson, 2011).

In addition to cameras, lidar, and radar, a number of other sensors may be used to help vehicles make sense of the world around them. Ultrasonic sensors can provide accurate short-range data (1–10 meters), which makes them useful for parking assistance systems and backup warning systems (Ford, 2013). They are also relatively inexpensive, with after-market solutions retailing for as little as $120. Infrared systems are capable of detecting lane markings without the lighting and environmental limitations of cameras. However, the range for this purpose is very small, making the systems more useful for detecting lane departures than for tracking lanes (Mathas, 2013). Infrared sensors may also be useful for detecting pedestrians and bicycles, particularly at night.

Sensor Suites

As this review suggests, each sensor provides different kinds of data and has its own limitations related to field of view, ambient operating conditions, and the elements in the environment that it can sense. Because the limitations of these sensors are fairly well understood, the usual practice is to construct suites of complementary sensors that are positioned around the vehicle to prevent blind spots—both visual blind spots (i.e., due to occluded views) and material blind spots (i.e., the inability to detect certain kinds of objects or certain properties of objects in the environment). Sensors can also be integrated to perceive more about the environment than can be learned purely from the sum of individual sensors' data. As one example, vision can detect colors of surfaces in the distance while lidar can be used to determine the material as that surface approaches. When coupled, a system can learn that green surfaces in the distance correspond to grass, allowing the vehicle to make greater sense of the environment that is far away (Thrun et al., 2007).

Vehicles also use sensor suites for localization, i.e., determining their own position in the world. The use of the global positioning systems (or GPS) is essential for localization. Vehicle GPS systems receive signals from orbiting satellites to triangulate their global coordinates. These coordinates are cross-referenced with maps of the road network to enable vehicles to identify their position on roads. The accuracy of GPS systems has improved significantly since 2000, when the U.S. government made GPS fully available to civilian users.[6] However, GPS error can still be large—several meters, even under ideal conditions. The errors grow rapidly when obstacles or terrain occlude the sky, preventing GPS receivers from obtaining signals from a sufficient number of satellites. This is a significant concern in urban areas, where skyscrapers create "urban canyons" in which GPS availability is severely limited.

---

[6] Prior to 2000, GPS used a system called "Selective Availability" that provided civilian applications with a degraded signal with lower accuracy than the military-grade signal. In May 2000, an executive order by President Bill Clinton (Exec. Order No. 12866) ended Selective Availability and provided civilian users the same quality signal as military users (National Coordination Office for Space-Based Positioning, Navigation, and Timing, 2014).

GPS is typically coupled with inertial navigation systems (INS), which consist of gyroscopes and accelerometers, to continuously calculate position, orientation, and velocity of a vehicle without need for external references. INS are used to improve the accuracy of GPS and to fill in "gaps" such as those caused by urban canyons. The key challenge with INS is drift—even over very short time periods, small errors can aggregate into large differences between calculated and true positions. For example, a 10-second period during which the system relies on INS because the GPS signal is unavailable can result in more than a meter of drift in calculated position, even with some of the most sophisticated systems (Applanix, 2012).

Thus, even these systems can result in inaccurate positioning. Many AVs therefore draw on prebuilt maps, which can come in many forms. For example, in the DARPA Urban Challenge, teams were given "Road Network Definition Files" that encoded approximate GPS coordinates for the course's road segments, stop signs, and waypoints. Many teams also manually corrected the definition files with aerial imagery of the road network to achieve more accurate positioning. Thus, vehicles could correct the error in their local pose estimates by correlating the location of features in the definition files with features they observed in the environment (Buehler, Iagnemma, and Singh, 2010). It may be difficult to construct and maintain highly accurate maps of all connected roads. This could limit the routes on which AVs drive.

Different combinations of sensors offer different combinations of capabilities and redundancies at different price-points, and cost is a key constraint. While every additional sensor may contribute some degree of navigational assistance in a particular set of conditions, it also increases the physical and computational complexity and cost of the vehicle, and decreases the feasibility of its introduction in commercial vehicles. Many sensor manufacturers are offering less sophisticated and lower-cost sensors tailored to particular needs.[7]

---

[7] As one example, Velodyne began offering a lidar with 32 lasers instead of 64 in response to customer demands for smaller size and lower cost ("Velodyne's LiDAR Division Doubles Production Capacity to Meet Demand," 2013).

There are also efforts to develop autonomous systems that use just a few low-cost sensors, but these systems have more operational limitations. MobilEye Vision Technologies, for example, has developed an AV that uses only cameras to drive in a single lane at highway speeds and identify and respond to traffic lights. "The idea is to get the best out of camera-only autonomous driving," noted one of MobilEye's executives (Markoff, 2013). Similarly, the winner of the 2013 Intel International Science and Engineering Fair, a 19-year-old student from Romania, developed an AV system design using radar and cameras at a cost of $4,000 per vehicle (Intel.com, 2013). At this point, it is not clear if there is a single suite of sensors that will emerge as the best tradeoff between the constraints of robustness of sensing and cost.

Environmental Challenges

Other challenges pose significant concerns. Certain ambient conditions (e.g., severe precipitation, dense fog) may pose problems for multiple sensors simultaneously. Common failure conditions such as this limit the extent to which sensor combinations can compensate for individual sensor limitations. It must be noted, however, that these same conditions pose problems for humans. Indeed, robotic sensors such as radar may prove more effective than human vision, and the rapid reaction of planning algorithms may be particularly valuable, making autonomous systems imperfect but potentially safer than human drivers in these adverse conditions.

Terrain also poses challenges. A sensor configuration appropriate for a flat environment may be inappropriate for steep hills, where sensors must look "up" or "down" slopes. Different terrain can require different sensor configurations, which may not be readily changeable. While sensors can be put on adjustable mounts to accommodate this problem, this adds complexity and cost (Urmson, Ragusa, et al., 2006).

Road materials also change from region to region. They are typically concrete and asphalt, but can be made of dirt, cobblestone, and other materials. Different materials have different reflectivity, and sensors calibrated to certain materials may have difficulty detecting other materials with equal fidelity.

Construction projects and roadwork are particularly difficult to negotiate, as there may be little consistency in signage and alerts, roadway materials may change suddenly and the maneuvers needed to navigate through construction zones may be complex and poorly marked. Moreover, these areas often involve deviations from preconstructed maps, so vehicle localization may be particularly difficult.

Each of these factors can have implications for where AVs can or cannot successfully operate. Weather and terrain vary significantly across the United States, as do the road materials and signage practices used by DOTs and other agencies. A vehicle that operates easily on flat terrain in Louisiana may have significant performance challenges on Colorado's snowy and steep roads, or in New York City's congested urban canyons.

Graceful Degradation

Sensor failure (as opposed to external environmental conditions) can also pose serious performance threats (Hwang et al., 2010). Sensors may fail because of electrical failures, physical damage, or age. It will be critical for AVs to have internal sensing and algorithms that can detect when internal components are not performing adequately. This is not easy. A sensor that fails to provide any data is easily detected as nonfunctioning, but a sensor that occasionally sends spurious data may be much harder to detect.

These and other failures will require a system that degrades gracefully (Berger and Rumpe, 2012). AVs will likely need to have an ultrareliable and simple low-level system that uses minimal sensor data to perform basic functions in the event of main system degradation or failure. The backup system must also be able to detect degradation and failure and override control rapidly and safely. The task of graceful degradation may be complicated by traffic conditions and roadways. If a system fails in the middle of a curve in dense traffic, it may need to be able to navigate to a safe area to pull over.

V2V and V2I Communication

Clearly, there are many challenges to overcome before vehicles can accurately perceive the state of the environment from sensor systems. Many researchers and developers have suggested an alternative: What if the environment communicated its state to the vehicle? This is the motivation behind V2V and V2I communication, in which vehicles communicate with the surrounding infrastructure, with each other, or both. In doing so, they could receive information about hazardous conditions, such as icy roads or crashes; nonhazardous conditions, such as congestions; or route recommendations. They could also coordinate their behavior—for example, by taking turns through intersections or maintaining faster speeds and closer spacing on highways.

These approaches have received significant attention in federally funded efforts; e.g., through the research programs of the Research and Innovative Technology Administration's (RITA's) Intelligent Transportation System Joint Program Office (Intelligent Transportation Systems, 2013a). A key part of the federally funded research effort—in partnership with industry and academia—is aimed at developing standards for Dedicated Short-Range Communication (DSRC) (Intelligent Transportation Systems, 2013b), bandwidth allocated by the FCC for automotive use (FCC, 1999). This spectrum is capable of supporting safety applications that require nearly instantaneous communication (Strickland, 2013). DSRC can enable a communication network of nodes consisting of mobile vehicles or roadside units, sharing traffic and safety information and coordinating vehicle behavior.

However, V2V and V2I have practical challenges, as well as technological challenges. Creating, maintaining, and ensuring ultra-reliability of public infrastructure for driverless cars may be prohibitively expensive, particularly in a time of growing fiscal uncertainty for transportation agencies. Additionally, to be safe and effective, V2V technologies require a critical level of deployment of vehicle communication technology, development of communication standards, and consistent application of those standards in platforms developed by different manufacturers. To coordinate behaviors, vehicles must also all be accurately localized before they can broadcast and coordinate their positions, velocities, and other features. There are also cybersecurity concerns. We discuss the issues raised by DSRC and communications more generally in Chapter Five.

Sharing the Drive

Partly as a result of all of the limitations listed above, a "shared driving" concept of operation is consistent with many expectations of the first commercially available AVs: vehicles can drive autonomously in certain operating conditions—e.g., below a particular speed, only on certain kinds of roads—and will revert to traditional, manual driving outside those boundaries or at the request of a human driver. Such shared driving conditions will depend little, if at all, on specially designed infrastructure or on the capabilities of other vehicles.

This approach poses its own challenges. One key challenge will be human driver reengagement. To experience most of the benefits of the technology, human drivers will need to be able to engage in other tasks while the vehicle is autonomously driving. For safety, however, they will need to quickly reengage at the request of the vehicle. Such context switching may need to occur fully and in a matter of seconds or less. Cognitive science research on distracted driving suggests this may be a significant safety challenge (Drews et al., 2009; Neubauer, Matthews, and Saxby, 2012). Finding the right balance between requiring the human to be ready to intervene at a moment's notice and realizing the benefits of this technology is likely to be a challenge.

For example, should the driver of a conditionally automated vehicle be encouraged or permitted to send a text or an email? Should the driver be able to watch a movie? And what should happen when humans almost inevitably rely too much upon the technology? Relatedly, there may be issues of consumer acceptance. While consumers may be willing to pay for a car that permits them to text or watch a movie while driving, they may be unwilling to pay much for automation that requires them to sit alert, hands on the wheel, ready to take over at any moment.

As with any other component of the driving system, the vehicle will need internal sensors to monitor the behavior of the human part of the system. Some have suggested a variety of mechanisms to ensure that the driver is sufficiently engaged—for example, a vibrating seat or wheel, or vehicle screens that show the road rather than entertainment. But while a vehicle manufacturer may carefully limit what is displayed on a vehicle's screen, it has little control over whether a consumer uses his own device to watch a movie or send messages. More active monitoring of the driver's behavior and attention is theoretically possible, but may be resisted by drivers.

The vehicle must also adapt gracefully when the human driver's performance is degraded; e.g., the driver is asleep or intoxicated. In these situations, the vehicle may refuse to engage in autonomous driving or fall back upon the backup system to bring the vehicle to a safe stop. This, in turn, may raise both engineering and privacy concerns. How will it be secure? With whom will it be shared? Will the data gathered about passengers be admissible evidence in trials? If the system mistakenly detects degraded driver performance, will there be a manual override? The legal implications of these technologies are complex and unclear.[8]

Similarly, developing the appropriate mental models for the collaboration necessary for automation Levels 2 and 3, where the driver needs to be prepared to take over, has yet to occur. While autopilots are familiar in both aviation and marine use, the marine and aviation contexts generally allow more time for transition between the autopilot and manual control—and in both cases, operators often receive extensive training about the capabilities and limitations of the systems.

Partly because many of the human-computer interaction issues outlined above are difficult, not everyone believes that Levels 2 and 3 autonomy and shared driving are the appropriate path. Some, for example, have advocated for fully autonomous, driverless vehicles that would travel at low speeds over a limited geographic area. Stanford

---

[8] As one example, the OnStar system uses a two-way mobile phone link to provide navigation assistance, in-vehicle security, remote engine shut-off, and other features. Such a system could be used by law enforcement to monitor conversations in the vehicle, to track the vehicle, or to allow dealerships to immobilize vehicles whose owners are past due in their payment. In September 2011, OnStar, a General Motors product, announced that it would continue collecting data from vehicles even if owners were no longer paying for the service, and left open the possibility of sharing or selling anonymized data (Poulsen, 2010; Li, 2013). After unfavorable media attention and congressional calls for a Federal Trade Commission investigation, GM reversed this policy and it was never implemented (Quain, 2011; Hill, 2011). However the data privacy issues raised by this incident remain unresolved with no clear consensus on the legality or ethics of companies' abilities to collect and extract value from user data.

University, for example, has plans to introduce a driverless shuttle on its campus, and the CityMobil 2 project in Europe will use low-speed driverless vehicles in a number of different European cities. Similarly, Singapore's Nanyang University plans to introduce a driverless low-speed shuttle on a 1.2-mile route (Coxworth, 2013). Such an approach sidesteps the difficult driver-computer interaction issues, though possibly at a cost of raising difficult pedestrian-computer interaction issues.

Integrity, Security, and Verification

AV software and hardware will be tested extensively, likely using many of the techniques used to test aircraft systems and other complex ultra-reliable systems. But virtually every consumer device, from cell phones to robotic vacuum cleaners, requires software upgrades. This creates software reliability challenges, as software upgrades may need to be backward-compatible with earlier models of vehicles and sensor systems. Moreover, as increasing numbers of vehicle models offer autonomous driving features, software and other system upgrades will have to perform on increasingly diverse platforms, making reliability and quality assurance all the more challenging.

Software upgrades highlight a broader concern with AVs: system security. Vehicles that are connected to each other, to infrastructure, or to the Internet are increasingly open to cyberattack. David Strickland, former head of NHTSA, has noted (2013):

> With this evolution comes increased challenges, primarily in the area of system reliability and cybersecurity—the latter growing more critical as vehicles are increasingly more connected to a wide variety of products . . . Whether the entry point into the vehicle is the Internet, aftermarket devices, USB ports, or mobile phones, these new portals bring new challenges.

Even primarily unconnected vehicles may be at risk. Software upgrades, for example, will likely require connection to the Internet, which creates the possibility of vehicles being attacked by computer viruses that corrupt the system; for example, a virus could enter the system by masquerading as a legitimate software upgrade. Preventing this requires extremely secure connections to upgrade servers and a number of "handshake" mechanisms to ensure that the source of upgrades—and the upgrades themselves—are legitimate and uncorrupted. Unchecked, malicious actors might be able to commandeer a single vehicle (or a fleet of vehicles) to commit crimes, or even acts of terrorism.

Software security is not the only concern. Vandals or criminals may use GPS jammers or send other interference signals to disrupt AV sensors or transmit false sensor readings to a vehicle's sensors; e.g., sending false lidar returns to a vehicle that is using three-dimensional mapping to navigate through its environment.[9] While this may be more difficult to achieve, it may also be more difficult to detect since spoofed sensor readings may appear legitimate.

Vehicle owners also pose possible security threats. Many technology enthusiasts seek access to their own systems to gain control over elements that are otherwise locked down by the manufacturer. The terms "jail breaking" and "rooting" refer to the act of breaching the built-in security for mobile phones (which is often accomplished through physical tampering) to provide the owner with greater access and flexibility; e.g., moving the phone from one carrier to another. AVs will surely be as big a temptation for "jail breaking" as users seek to improve performance or run their own software, almost certainly while risking safety. This will require manufacturers to ensure users cannot hack into the vehicle's hardware and software systems. It may also require states to perform annual inspections of the vehicle system's integrity.

A mobile communications provider we interviewed stated that security issues are not well understood. His concern was that, as vehicles become more computerized and more connected, they provide another aspect of critical infrastructure and a potential target for a cyberattack. He said all of an AV's systems ought to be designed to resist possible intrusion by hackers, citing an example where hackers were able to access a car's electronic systems through a seemingly innocuous system to monitor tire pressure. He said security measures need to apply to all

---

[9]   However, human drivers are not immune to such attacks and could be blinded by lasers or misled by false signs.

communications paths into the car, whether it is Wi-Fi, cellular communications, or DSRC.

Like any technology, AVs will experience failures and breaches. The most critical feature will be the system's ability to detect failures and breaches and act safely—switching to a tightly controlled and simple safety system or refusing to engage at all.

Policy Implications

The variety of AV development efforts suggest that states may soon face the question of whether and how to regulate vehicles with different capabilities and operating limitations. Different manufacturers may take vastly different approaches to autonomous driving. Google, for example, seems to be pursuing a vehicle that is fully autonomous and capable of complex and general driving, while MobilEye seems focused on a narrower driving capability. The same manufacturer may offer different models or different capabilities in new versions of the same vehicle model. This has implications for state and national regulations, vehicle standards, liability, and near-term DOT investments. We touch on these issues briefly here, and discuss them further in later chapters.

Policymakers could regulate different specific vehicle capabilities: highway vs. city driving, fast vs. slow driving, fully autonomous vs. driver back-up capabilities. As stakeholder interviews suggest, it is likely prohibitively expensive for individual state or local agencies to develop and enforce numerous regulations tailored to specific operating conditions and capabilities.

Policymakers must also consider how to regulate the drivers of different AVs to ensure they understand how to safely operate and interact with the machines. This human factor is critical to the safety for vehicles that use a shared driving concept. Many states already require specific tests and certifications to drive motorcycles, for example, and they have limitations (principally age restrictions) on who may drive them. Regulations for drivers of AVs could take a similar approach, requiring additional practical tests to demonstrate drivers' operational competence. Yet, different AV models and capabilities may each require different kinds of interactions with the driver, making it difficult to develop a single standardized test until AV standards are in place.

Alternatively, policymakers may forgo practical testing of drivers or vehicles entirely. They may instead rely on manufacturers or third parties to ensure vehicle safety and to ensure that the driver has been properly trained in using the vehicle and understands its limitations. Policymakers may additionally require drivers and/or manufacturers to hold additional insurance to bear liability for crashes. These approaches may shield transportation agencies from costs and liability, but they will not necessarily lead to greater road safety. As we discuss in Chapter Three, different states are using different approaches to navigate these complex regulatory aims.

The diversity of vehicle capabilities, and of the ways in which vehicles may suffer failures, also suggest that safety and performance standards for AVs will be significantly different from those of traditional vehicles. Standards may specify capability requirements focused on sensing different objects in the environment under different conditions, system redundancy, graceful degradation, emergency behaviors, physical safety, and software and communication integrity. We discuss standards in Chapter Seven.

Finally, there are some opportunities for transportation agencies to take near-term actions to increase AV safety. Currently, while DOTs have codes for signage and markings, these are sometimes not conformed to in practice. This poses challenges for vehicle perception and navigation, particularly through construction areas or irregular routes. DOTs could require stricter conformance to road signage and marking standards to make the perception challenge easier. Standardization across states would also be significantly beneficial; not only for AV owners but also conventional drivers who sometimes struggle to understand confusing detour markings.

Similarly, transportation agencies could further maintain and provide online, real-time, detailed records of construction and other variations in the transportation system. Such information could leverage the record-keeping that transportation agencies already use, but would be more widespread than existing record systems, which focus on highways, and provide a higher level of detail. Such efforts would aid both AVs and human drivers who could use such up-to-date information for real-time route planning.

Conclusion

AVs have been an area of research for many decades. Efforts of the last 15 years, first by universities and then by industry, have brought this technology to near readiness. Deployment still faces several challenges, however. Perception of the environment remains the biggest challenge to reliable driving. New nondriving challenges have also emerged, such as ensuring system security and integrity.

In the near term, manufacturers are likely to develop vehicles with significantly different capabilities. These have a number of policy implications, including the challenge for policymakers to regulate many diverse vehicles with different operating constraints, and to ensure that drivers understand these vehicles' capabilities and can operate them safely.

CHAPTER FIVE

The Role of Telematics and Communications

In this chapter, we discuss the role of telematics to enabling autonomous vehicle technology. First, we discuss the key telematics technology applications that may be used in autonomous vehicles. After discussing why these technologies are important, and the potential technical and public policy issues raised by telematics, we address specific stakeholder concerns and policy issues.

Telematics, the transfer of data to and from a moving vehicle, will be increasingly important to the future of autonomous vehicle technology for several reasons. First, at least one important vision of autonomous vehicle technology relies upon telematics to continually update the "state of the world" upon which vehicles rely. Google recently purchased Waze, a company that creates such maps and is expected to integrate it into its design for autonomous vehicles. The central advantage to such an approach is that such maps can be continually updated in real-time by any cars using this system (Goel, 2013). By crowd-sourcing data collection, Waze sidesteps some of the issues with the use of a static map. Suppose, for example, that some obstruction in the roadway is created by a spill from a truck. Once information about that obstruction is sensed by one car using this system, information about it can be nearly instantaneously communicated to every other car using the same system.

Second, the federal government has supported the development of Dedicated Short-Range Communications (DSRC), by dedicating bandwidth of the electromagnetic spectrum to this purpose, to allow vehicle-to-vehicle (V2V) and vehicle-to-infrastructure (V2I) applications. These applications would permit direct communications (unmediated by the Internet) of vehicles and vehicles to infrastructure. It is possible that if one car's sensors malfunctioned, it could temporarily rely on the sensors of nearby vehicles in order to safely maneuver. This is called "sensor virtualization" and might add a level of redundancy in case of sensor failure.

Third, even apart from addressing some of the technological problems of autonomy, many of the stakeholders with whom we spoke mentioned the inevitable need to send software updates to consumers. Currently, OEMs face two costly and not very effective choices: ask customers to return to the dealership for a software update or send a "thumb drive" containing the software updates to all customers. The need to update on-board technology raises the complex issue of secure communications and data transfer.

Finally, many of the stakeholders with whom we spoke emphasized the importance of communications and telematics to enable "infotainment." Increasingly complex and interactive forms of entertainment pose considerable safety risks in a conventionally operated car that relies upon the driver. However, the availability of such infotainment, taking advantage of screens much larger than those of a smartphone, may help increase consumer demand for autonomous vehicle technology. According to some of our interviewees, the ability to watch a movie or write an email are examples of what consumer research has identified as key selling points for Level 3 or Level 4 autonomous technology. Stakeholders from two different global high-technology companies, a global wireless communications executive and a senior executive at a telematics company, stated that they expect a synergistic effect between in-vehicle infotainment and AV technology—each increasing demand for the other.

However, there is considerable uncertainty about the technology—or the combinations of technology—by which automobiles will communicate with the Internet, with other vehicles, and with transportation infrastructure. In the next sections, we will review the communications technologies used by AVs, explore the insights provided by key stakeholders, and examine the technological and policy issues posed by wireless communications and spectrum availability.

A Review of the Communications Technologies Used by Autonomous Vehicles

The following section will provide a brief explanation of different technologies and identify how they are used in AVs. All of these technologies use radio frequency (RF) spectrum.[1]

Commercial Wireless Services

One possible platform for AV voice and data communications is via commercial wireless services. Mobile phone usage is widespread throughout the world. The frequencies used for commercial wireless services—cellular, Global System for Mobile Communications (GSM), Personal Communications Service (PCS), 3G, 4G—are generally below 3 gigahertz (GHz) (Kelly and Johnson, 2012, p. 1280).[2]

Vehicle telematics applications, such as General Motors OnStar, use commercial cellular services for voice and data communications. According to media reports, Chrysler recently signed an agreement with Sprint Nextel to add its UConnect system to several vehicles. UConnect pulls data through either an embedded data connection or a smartphone (Newcomb, 2012). In *Business Week*, Fitchard (2012) noted that "two of the biggest connected-car platforms, Ford's Sync and Cadillac's CUE, depend on drivers using their own smartphones to link their apps to the network." Fitchard argued that relying upon users' phones was probably the right choice:

---

[1]   Radio spectrum refers to the part of the electromagnetic spectrum corresponding to radio frequencies—that is, frequencies lower than around 300 GHz (or, equivalently, wavelengths longer than about 1 mm). Different parts of the radio spectrum are used for different radio transmission technologies and applications. Radio spectrum is typically government regulated in developed countries and, in some cases, is sold or licensed to operators of private radio transmission systems (for example, cellular telephone operators or broadcast television stations). Ranges of allocated frequencies are often referred to by their provisioned use (for example, cellular spectrum or television spectrum).

[2]   The primary bands in the United States are at 700 megahertz (MHz), 800 MHz, 1.8–1.9 GHz, 1.4 GHz, 1.7 GHz, 2.1 GHz, and 2.4–2.6 GHz. Mobile phones used in Europe, Latin America, and elsewhere operate in the 400 MHz, 800 MHz, 900 MHz, 1.8 GHz, and 1.9 GHz bands.

[C]onsumers trade in their smartphones for more sophisticated models every 18 months. Any radio, processor, or platform technology an automaker embeds in a car could become obsolete within a few years . . . New smartphones will be able to take advantage of those improvements in speed, capacity, and efficiency, while the radios embedded in the chassis of your car will not.

Long Term Evolution, marketed as 4G LTE, is a standard for wireless data communications technology and an evolution of the GSM/UMTS (Universal Mobile Telecommunications System) standards. The goal of LTE was to increase the capacity and speed of wireless data networks using new digital signal processing techniques and modulations that were developed around 2000. The LTE wireless interface is incompatible with 2G and 3G networks, so that it must be operated in a separate wireless spectrum. The LTE standard covers a range of many different bands, each of which is designated by both a frequency and a band number. As a result, phones from one country may not work in other countries.

This creates a potential challenge for General Motors, which claims that it will provide the largest deployment of 4G LTE in the auto industry, with the rollout in 2014 of Chevrolet, Cadillac, Buick, and GMC 2015 models (Amend, 2013). AT&T will provide the LTE connectivity, which GM will overlay on the OnStar technology already deployed on approximately 6 million vehicles. It will be available as part of an OnStar package, or possibly as a subscription independent from the telematics service, according to media reports (Amend, 2013). According to news reports, GM expects widespread in-vehicle 4G LTE connectivity to spur V2I communications, thus enhancing safety, efficiency, and convenience for drivers and passengers. The technology also would make services such as real-time traffic and navigation updates possible, according to GM (Amend, 2013).

Similarly, Audi announced that its 2013 Audi A3 features 4G LTE wireless connectivity supplied by Qualcomm Technologies' second-generation multi-mode 3G/4G LTE chipset (Day, 2013). According to media reports, the "Audi connect" services in the A3 are expected to provide features such as an in-car Wi-Fi hotspot, Internet radio, Web services, and an augmented navigation system that presents street-level visual imagery streamed to the vehicle (Day, 2013).

Dedicated Short-Range Communications

DSRC is a short-range (less than 1,000 meters) wireless service specifically created to be the wireless link for V2V and vehicle-to-roadside infrastructure (FCC, 2004, paragraph 23).[3] DSRC is intended to enable short-range wireless communications both between vehicles and between vehicles and roadside infrastructure—to support, especially, safety applications such as intersection collision avoidance (see Figure 5.1). DSRC is also available for nonsafety messages, vehicle diagnostics, and even commercial transactions (Kelly and Johnson, 2012, p. 1282).

DSRC has been central to the DOT's efforts to develop connected vehicles. However, DSRC also has been subject to some controversy, as

Figure 5.1
Uses for DSRC

In forward obstacle detection and avoidance, a DSRC channel is used to communicate traffic information backward through vehicles to alert drivers of possible problems up to thousands of feet ahead of them. This communication can enhance the functionality of adaptive cruise control systems. For emergency vehicle warnings, DSRC would enable information to relay forward through traffic, which could clear the way for the emergency vehicle and reduce risks to other drivers.

Forward obstacle detection and avoidance

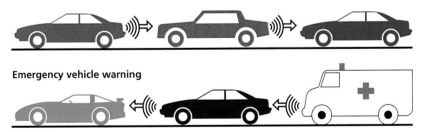

Emergency vehicle warning

SOURCE: "Dedicated Short Range Communications," undated.
RAND RR443-5.1

---

[3]   See also Kelly and Johnson, 2012, p. 1281.

a result of the lack of current applications for it. Indeed, one major technology company cited DSRC as a paradigmatic example of how *not* to develop a new technology and the risks of government involvement. As explained in more detail below, the FCC is considering allowing unlicensed uses for this spectrum, which is the subject of considerable debate concerning potential interference issues with DSRC.

Bluetooth

Bluetooth is a wireless technology standard for exchanging data over short distances (using short-wavelength radio transmissions) from fixed and mobile devices, creating personal area networks with high levels of security. The technology enables mobile phones brought into a vehicle to route incoming and outgoing calls through the vehicle, creating a hands-free wireless phone (Kelly and Johnson, 2012, p. 1284). In the United States and Europe, Bluetooth operates at 2400 to 2483.5 MHz, divided into 79 1 MHz channels (Kelly and Johnson, 2012, p. 1284). In Japan, Bluetooth operates at 2472 to 2497 MHz (Kelly and Johnson, 2012). While it is primarily used in automobiles to extend the capabilities of wireless phones, it may also be used as a way of facilitating communications of the vehicle itself, either by enabling V2I communications or by transmitting data to a wireless phone for retransmission.

Wi-Fi

Wi-Fi is a popular technology that allows an electronic device to exchange data wirelessly (using radio spectrum) over a computer network, including high-speed Internet connections. In the United States, the 2.4 GHz band is the primary band for Wi-Fi use, although the 5.2 GHz and 5.3 GHz bands have also been allocated for wireless broadband access (Kelly and Johnson, 2012, p. 1283).

On January 9, 2013, the FCC announced a governmentwide effort to increase speed and reduce congestion in Wi-Fi networks by releasing up to 195 MHz of spectrum in the 5 GHz band—the largest block of unlicensed spectrum to be made available for the expansion of Wi-Fi and other devices that use unlicensed spectrum since 2003. Stakeholders in connected and AV development raised the concern that the FCC's release of spectrum in the 5 GHz band to unlicensed users could impede the development of the DSRC network. Stakeholders urged the FCC to wait until the conclusion of current DSRC testing in Ann Arbor, Mich., and until NHTSA issues a regulatory decision (Intelligent Transportation Society of America, 2013).

Stakeholder Viewpoints on Autonomous Vehicle Communications

The Research and Innovative Technology Administration of the U.S. DOT characterized its vision of "connected cars" as requiring communications in the following way: "a wireless communications network that includes cars, buses, trucks, trains, traffic signals, cell phones, and other devices. Like the Internet, which provides information connectivity, connected vehicle technology provides a starting point for transportation connectivity that will potentially enable countless applications and spawn new industries" (Intelligent Transportation Systems, 2013b). Specifically, the U.S. DOT envisions connected vehicle applications that will provide connectivity

- among vehicles to enable crash prevention
- between vehicles and the infrastructure to enable safety, mobility, and environmental benefits
- among vehicles, infrastructure, and wireless devices to provide continuous, real-time connectivity to all system users (Intelligent Transportation Systems, 2013b).

In 1999, the FCC approved DSRC to be the wireless link for V2V and V2I communications. This communications network was central to the U.S. DOT's vision of connected vehicles. In 2004, the FCC enacted the technical and service regulations for DSRC. Although DSRC licenses became available in 2004, the deployment to date has been limited to experimental and demonstrative projects. The most prominent of these is a "Safety Pilot Study" in Ann Arbor, Mich., which involves more than 3,000 vehicles and will evaluate "connected vehicle" technologies, particularly DSRC (Intelligent Transportation

Systems, 2013b). A report concerning the findings of the safety pilot study is expected by the end of 2013 (Intelligent Transportation Society of America, 2013).

Many of the stakeholders we interviewed described a convergence of communications and sensor-based technologies to enable AV operation. Stakeholders cited the limitations of sensor-only solutions (not cost-effective for mass-market adoption, lack of 360-degree mapping of environments) and DSRC-only solutions (DSRC-based V2I may require significant infrastructure investment and a government mandate to require new cars to have DSRC and older models to be retrofitted). A global provider of technology solutions we spoke with is working with automakers to develop communications platforms whether they are "built into the car or brought into the car." This stakeholder described three computing environments that create a horizontal communications platform for AVs: (1) the car, (2) the technology brought into the car, and (3) the Internet "cloud," all of which need to work well together. He noted that different OEMs have distinctly different viewpoints about integrating communications platforms into a car: General Motors has announced that it will be integrating an LTE connection into all of its 2014 vehicles, whereas Ford has publicly described GM's integration of LTE as a "mistake," because integrating any technology into a car that lasts for 10 years is certain to become outdated. He also explained that the "customer experience" is becoming a more significant part of the automobile purchase decision, and said the big challenge is to "merge infotainment and mission-critical," in terms of new communications platforms.

Another stakeholder we interviewed, who works with onboard navigation systems for OEMs, confirmed the importance of communications capabilities in new car sales. He explained that when potential customers are polled about what they want in "connected cars" or "autonomous vehicles," their response is that they want to use a personal smartphone to obtain data for navigation, to have email read aloud to the driver, to send SMS (text) messages by voice, and to have text messages read back aloud for the driver. Customers also want the ability to demand navigation to a very specific retail outlet, such as "find me a gas station that sells diesel fuel," rather than simply "find me a gas station."

This stakeholder explained that a major consumer criticism of cars at the moment is that even new cars have old navigation systems and maps, because of the manufacturing time. According to this stakeholder, navigation systems are generally three to five years out of date when cars come off the line, and updating them is expensive. It requires either sending the customer a USB drive with updates, or customers returning to the dealership. This issue would apply to updating onboard communications systems, as well. This stakeholder confirmed that industry research showed that customers want to move seamlessly among their home laptop, PC, or iPad; their car screen; and their smartphone. This analysis was supported by a media expert who is working on radio applications that will cross all three environments. One of the global technology developers we interviewed acknowledged that preparing a communications platform for "infotainment" in vehicles was perceived to be the gateway for his company into many other aspects of autonomous car communications.

Many stakeholders concurred that the marketing advantage provided by safety devices such as Advanced Driver Assist Systems and the "customer experience" benefits provided by "infotainment" systems were likely to require a convergence of technologies in AVs. As one stakeholder commented, communications should be viewed through the lens of "what are the potential inhibitors or accelerators for deployment" of AVs. A global technology developer described how a DSRC-only solution might inhibit mass-market deployment for up to 30 years, but a combined approach of sensors, radar, lidar, and DSRC could accelerate deployment of AVs by bringing costs down for mass-market acceptance. Groupe Speciale Mobile, a European-based organization of global mobile-technology providers, confirmed the viewpoint expressed by many stakeholders (Amend, 2013) and estimates that 20 percent of global vehicle sales in 2015 will include embedded connectivity, while 50 percent will be either embedded or capable of linking with a smartphone. By 2025, the organization says, every car sold will be connected by multiple means (Amend, 2013). All of the stakeholders we interviewed agreed that communications and telematics are essential features of AVs, though there was some disagreement about the specific means (e.g., DSRC, LTE) by which this communication would occur, and the extent to which it is necessary for an AV to rely on data received from other cars.

Spectrum Issues for Autonomous Vehicles

In this section, we discuss policy issues regarding the allocation of spectrum.

Who Regulates It?

The communication technologies described in the previous section all use radio frequency spectrum. Generally, it is difficult for these applications to use the same frequencies at the same time, due to interference issues. In order to avoid interference, spectrum is divided up into bands that are allocated to one or more services.[4] The demand for use of spectrum has increased exponentially, as devices that require a significant amount of spectrum to operate, such as broadband networks, streaming video, smartphones, and tablets have become widespread throughout the United States and the world.

In the United States, spectrum use is regulated by two agencies, the National Telecommunications and Information Agency (NTIA), which governs the use of spectrum by federal government agencies and departments, and the FCC, which regulates interstate and international communications by radio, television, wire, satellite, and cable in all 50 states, the District of Columbia, and U.S. territories. Both agencies are engaged in spectrum allocation issues, in part because of recent legislation, the Middle Class Tax Relief and Job Creation Act of 2012, that requires NTIA and the FCC to investigate how to use spectrum more efficiently (Public Law 112-96, §6406).

---

[4]   For a discussion of the relevant property rights and ways that the private sector might reallocate them, see Yoo (2012).

Will Spectrum Regulation Affect the Deployment of Autonomous Vehicles?

All of the technologies that have been discussed in the previous section except Wi-Fi and Bluetooth operate in *licensed* spectrum, which has to be authorized by the FCC (FCC, undated a). The FCC has the authority pursuant to Title III of the Communications Act of 1934, as amended, to allocate spectrum for use by private, commercial, and state and local government authorities (U.S. Code, 1934). Recently, the FCC's proposal to release up to 195 GHz of spectrum in the 5.9 GHz band raised concerns about implications of this action for DSRC and AVs (FCC, 2013). Specifically, the Intelligent Transportation Society of America (ITS America), which represents major automotive manufacturers and technology companies, stated in a February 12, 2013, letter to then-FCC Chairman Julius Genachowski that

> We share NTIA's concern about the potential risks associated with introducing a substantial number of unlicensed devices into the 5.9 GHz band on which connected vehicle systems are based, and support NTIA's conclusion that further analysis is needed to determine whether and how the multiple risk factors could be mitigated. We furthermore agree that "the FCC and NTIA must determine that licensed users will be protected by technical solutions and that the primary mission of federal spectrum users will not be compromised before adopting service rules authorizing U-NII devices" to operate in the band.

A majority of the stakeholders we interviewed believe that AVs will use a combination of the communications technologies described in the previous section, including DSRC. Therefore, the regulation of licensed spectrum and the uses allowed for unlicensed spectrum are important factors in AV deployment.

How Will the FCC Proceed to Make Decisions Concerning DSRC Spectrum?

The FCC's decisionmaking process is governed by the Administrative Procedure Act (U.S. Code, 1994, §§553–557), which is the federal statute that designates the way in which administrative agencies of the federal government of the United States may propose and establish regulations. The Administrative Procedure Act also sets up a process for the U.S. federal courts to directly review agency decisions (U.S. Code, 1994, §§553–557).

The current FCC proceeding that concerns DSRC is a Notice of Proposed Rulemaking (NPRM), "Revision of Part 15 of the Commission's Rules to Permit Unlicensed National Information Infrastructure (U-NII) Devices in the 5 GHz Bands" (FCC, 2013), or "the U-NII proceeding." Most FCC rules are adopted by a process known as "notice and comment" rulemaking. Under that process, the FCC gives the public notice that it is considering adopting or modifying rules on a particular subject and seeks the public's comment (FCC, undated b).

In the U-NII proceeding, the language that pertains to DSRC states, "we also seek comment on making available an additional 195 megahertz of spectrum in the 5.35–5.47 GHz and 5.85–5.925 GHz bands for U-NII use. This could increase the spectrum available to unlicensed devices in the 5 GHz band by approximately 35 percent and would represent a significant increase in the spectrum available for unlicensed devices across the overall radio spectrum." Specifically, the FCC is considering changes to its Part 15 rules. Part 302(a) of the Communications Act of 1934 gives the Commission authority "consistent with the public interest, convenience and necessity" to make "reasonable regulations" that concern devices that use radio frequency spectrum.

How Will the FCC Weigh Competing Claims Concerning Spectrum Use?

The U-NII proceeding proposes to open up the 5 GHz band to unlicensed devices, specifically the frequency band between 5.850 and 5.925 GHz, which is currently allocated to DSRC. A review of the U-NII proceeding commenters and their positions is instructive. A large number of FCC rulemakings concern industry members who advocate different outcomes, based on their commercial interests. In this proceeding, however, industry members such as Ford, the Auto Alliance and the Association of Global Automakers, and ITS America have been joined by federal and state agencies, departments and associations such as the National Transportation Safety Board (NTSB), NTIA, the U.S. DOT, the California Department of Transportation (Caltrans), the Arizona DOT, and the American Association of State Highway and Transportation Officials (AASHTO).

The comments presented by the U.S. DOT emphasized DSRC's importance to public safety, citing statistics about how DSRC is likely to significantly reduce the 30,000 American lives lost each year in automobile accidents. According to U.S. DOT, there were 32,367 fatalities and approximately 2,200,000 injuries in 2011 for an estimated 5,338,000 crashes resulting in billions of dollars in cost to society in the United States (NHTSA, 2012b). NTSB, Caltrans, the Arizona DOT, AASHTO, ITS America, Ford Motor Company, and the Alliance of Automobile Manufacturers all filed comments cautioning the FCC about the substantial technical, policy, economic, and practical challenges of allowing unlicensed devices to use the DSRC's 5.9 GHz band. U.S. DOT's comments stated, "[t]here is insufficient information about how U-NII devices would detect DSRC devices, and how U-NII devices would yield access to the channels within the 5850–5925 MHz band. Therefore, we cannot accurately and reliably assess the impacts on sharing in the 5850–5925 MHz band at this time. As a result, we are concerned that taking steps toward a sharing scheme would jeopardize safety" (U.S. DOT, 2013, p. 4).

The FCC, not Congress, included the DSRC spectrum in the U-NII NPRM. Congress directed in §6406 of the Middle Class Tax Relief and Jobs Act of 2012 (hereafter referred to as §6406) that "the Commission shall begin a proceeding to modify part 15 of title 47, Code of Federal Regulations, to allow unlicensed U-NII devices to operate in the *5350–5470 MHz band*" (Public Law 112-96). It did not state that the FCC proceeding should include the *5850–5925 MHz band*, which is the band assigned to DSRC.[5] The U-NII NPRM recognizes the precise assignment from Congress, stating, "the initiation

---

5   SEC. 6406. UNLICENSED USE IN THE 5 GHZ BAND.

(a) MODIFICATION OF COMMISSION REGULATIONS TO ALLOW CERTAIN UNLICENSED USE.—

(1) IN GENERAL.—Subject to paragraph (2), not later than 1 year after the date of the enactment of this Act, the Commission shall begin a proceeding to modify part 15 of

of this proceeding satisfies the requirements of §6406(a) of the 'Middle Class Tax Relief and Job Creation Act of 2012,' which requires the Commission to begin a proceeding to modify part 15 of title 47, Code of Federal Regulations, to allow unlicensed U-NII devices to operate in the 5350–5470 MHz band" (FCC, 2013, paragraph 2).

Section 6406 also directed the Assistant Secretary of NTIA, in consultation with the Department of Defense and other affected agencies, to conduct a study evaluating known and proposed spectrum-sharing technologies and the risk to federal users if unlicensed U-NII devices were allowed to operate in the 5350–5470 MHz band and in the 5850–5925 MHz band. NTIA submitted a letter to the FCC in the U-NII proceeding, warning of risks to federal users if the FCC allows

---

title 47, Code of Federal Regulations, to allow unlicensed U-NII devices to operate in the 5350–5470 MHz band.

(2) REQUIRED DETERMINATIONS.—The Commission may make the modification described in paragraph (1) only if the Commission, in consultation with the Assistant Secretary, determines that—

(A) licensed users will be protected by technical solutions, including use of existing, modified, or new spectrum sharing technologies and solutions, such as dynamic frequency selection; and

(B) the primary mission of Federal spectrum users in the 5350–5470 MHz band will not be compromised by the introduction of unlicensed devices.

(b) STUDY BY NTIA.—

(1) IN GENERAL.—The Assistant Secretary, in consultation with the Department of Defense and other impacted agencies, shall conduct a study evaluating known and proposed spectrum sharing technologies and the risk to Federal users if unlicensed U-NII devices were allowed to operate in the 5350–5470 MHz band and in the 5850–5925 MHz band.

(2) SUBMISSION.—The Assistant Secretary shall submit to the Commission and the Committee on Energy and Commerce of the House of Representatives and the Committee on Commerce, Science, and Transportation of the Senate—

(A) not later than 8 months after the date of the enactment of this Act, a report on the portion of the study required by paragraph (1) with respect to the 5350–5470 MHz band; and (B) not later than 18 months after the date of the enactment of this Act, a report on the portion of the study required by paragraph (1) with respect to the 5850–5925 MHz band.

(c) DEFINITIONS.—In this section:

(1) 5350–5470 MHZ BAND.—The term "5350–5470 MHz band" means the portion of the electromagnetic spectrum between the frequencies from 5350 megahertz to 5470 megahertz.

(2) 5850–5925 MHZ BAND.—The term "5850–5925 MHz band" means the portion of the electromagnetic spectrum between the frequencies from 5850 megahertz to 5925 megahertz.

U-NII devices to operate in the 5350–5470 MHz and 5850–5925 MHz bands (Nebbia, 2013). Specifically, NTIA's letter stated that, "our report identified a number of risks to FCC-authorized intelligent transport system stations operating Dedicated Short Range Communications Service (DSRC) systems in the 5850–5925 MHz band and suggested mitigation strategies. Some of the key intelligent transportation system applications will perform important public safety functions by acting to prevent the majority of types of roadway crashes." The Arizona and California DOTs supported the safety concerns expressed by U.S. DOT and NTIA in letters to the FCC.

The FCC will have to address the issues raised by U.S. DOT, NTIA, and the Arizona and California DOTs in issuing its final rule. It also will have to consider its own precedent in establishing DSRC. As U.S. DOT's comments pointed out, "in 1999, the FCC allocated 75 megahertz of spectrum in the 5.850–5.925 GHz band to support [intelligent transport systems] and DSRC upon which V2V and V2I depend" (U.S. DOT, 2013, p. 2).[6] At that time, the Commission explained that the decision to set aside this spectrum for intelligent transport systems would "further the goals of the United States . . . Congress and the Department of Transportation to improve the efficiency of the Nation's transportation infrastructure" (U.S. DOT, 2013, p. 2, citing 1999 Order paragraph 1.1). DOT cited the FCC's determinations in its 1999 Report and Order that the 5.9 GHz band allocation would "ensure that adequate spectrum will be available for advanced DSRC applications that are anticipated in the future," including highway systems requiring "dedicated wideband channels to ensure service reliability" (U.S. DOT, 2013, p. 2, citing 1999 Order paragraph 1.9).

In brief, the FCC may be in a difficult position in issuing a final rule in this NPRM concerning the 5.9 GHz band assigned to DSRC. It will have to balance the demands of the various stakeholders in the commercial wireless industry and the pressure from Congress to make

---

6   See the FCC's Report and Order, ET Docket No. 98-95, *Amendment of Parts 2 and 90 of the Commission's Rules to Allocate the 5.850–5.925 GHz Band to the Mobile Service for Dedicated Short Range Communications of Intelligent Transportation Services* (Oct. 21, 2009) (1999 Order).

additional spectrum available for use, with the risks to public safety expressed by federal and state agencies and departments that are experts on public safety issues. The FCC also will have to consider the $450 million that the U.S. DOT intelligent transport systems program has invested in researching and developing technology and applications to use the DSRC spectrum (U.S. DOT, 2013, p. 3), and how uncertainty about the future of DSRC could derail the auto industry's progress toward the public safety benefits of DSRC described by U.S. DOT and other federal and state agencies and departments.

Several paths exist for the FCC in dealing with DSRC as part of this NPRM. First, rulemaking can take up to five years, in which time additional evidence and factors may be added to the record, making it easier to discern the way forward (McGarity, 1992). The FCC could choose not to proceed with its rulemaking at all, but then it would have to address the congressional mandate of §6406(a). Another approach could be to defer the examination of the risks to users in the 5.9 GHz band assigned to DSRC until after a second report from NTIA has been completed and filed with the FCC and the U.S. Senate Committee on Commerce, Science and Transportation, as required by §6406(b). The FCC could defer an examination of the 5.9 GHz band indefinitely, since this band was not included in §6406(a). Another possible outcome is that if and when the FCC issues a rule, participants in the U-NII proceeding might seek reconsideration at the FCC or seek appellate review at the U.S. Court of Appeals for the District of Columbia Circuit, which would further delay any final outcome.[7]

There are competing claims to spectrum use, as exemplified by this NPRM. The FCC must weigh these competing claims and evaluate what best serves the public interest.

---

[7] Parties that disagree with a final rule or the FCC's accompanying analysis may file a petition for reconsideration explaining why the FCC was wrong. Alternatively, parties to the NPRM who disagree with a rule that affects them may seek review by a federal appellate court. In the majority of cases, this will be the U.S. Court of Appeals for the District of Columbia Circuit (FCC, undated b).

Spectrum Policy Issues

How important is preserving the 5.9 GHz band exclusively for DSRC in the use of AVs? We interviewed executives of a major auto manufacturer, who said the OEMs are "in unison about the need" for DSRC. This statement is supported by joint comments to the U-NII NPRM that were filed jointly at the FCC by the Alliance of Automobile Manufacturers and the Association of Global Automakers,[8] which together represent the manufacturers of approximately 99 percent of all cars and light trucks sold in the United States. The joint comments, which contained 34 pages and a 28-page Technical Appendix, support the need for interference-free spectrum in the 5.9 GHz DSRC band. Specifically, the joint comments state that

> the Alliance and Global are skeptical that, as proposed by the Commission, U-NII devices will be able to share, or operate in close proximity to, the 5.9 GHz DSRC band without causing severe and persistent, harmful interference to DSRC vehicle-to vehicle ("V2V") and vehicle-to infrastructure ("V2I") communications. U-NII use of the 5.9 GHz band could cause harmful co-channel, adjacent channel, and out-of-band interference to DSRC services. This interference would degrade DSRC V2V and V2I communication, make it impossible to confidently develop new latency-sensitive safety and other applications requiring high spectrum availability, and call into question the viability of the U.S. Department of Transportation's and auto industry's shared vision for connected vehicles.[9]

On the other hand, most of our interviewees were in the transportation community and may have an understandable interest in preserving this spectrum for transportation use. It is not clear exactly how much connectivity self-driving vehicles will require—the Google AV, for example, has not relied on extensive connectivity. Further, if AVs

---

[8] See comments of the Alliance of Automobile Manufacturers, Inc., and the Association of Global Automakers in FCC (2013), p. 1.

[9] See comments of the Alliance of Automobile Manufacturers, Inc., and the Association of Global Automakers, Inc., in FCC (2013), p. iv.

do need connectivity, it is not clear that it has to be in this particular band. And finally, even if AVs do need—or simply benefit from—the 5.9 GHz band, dispositive tests have not yet shown that they cannot share spectrum with unlicensed devices.

The FCC, therefore, faces a critical choice between supporting enhanced Internet access and preventing potentially harmful interference to DSRC spectrum if it is shared by unlicensed devices. This dilemma will persist until the effects of spectrum sharing in the 5.9 GHz band have been clearly demonstrated. The FCC will need to determine which course better serves the "public interest," as expressed in the Communications Act of 1934.

Several stakeholders stated that there has to be a "multistakeholder solution" to spectrum issues. A global wireless communications provider we interviewed stated that "an autonomous car is still going to be a connected car." This stakeholder maintains that as AV technology improves, it will spur further demand for connectivity anyway, because drivers will have more time and attention available for things other than focusing on the road. For mobile communications carriers, this means increasing demand for spectrum to support voice and video applications. The FCC's policymaking in the current proceeding concerning the 5.9 GHz band may have far-reaching implications that will either accelerate or inhibit deployment of DSRC and AVs.

Internet access is an important aspect of daily life and business, but DSRC can assist in preventing crash deaths on a major scale. While some have expressed concern about the lack of development of DSRC applications to date, it seems premature to make a decision about the use of the spectrum that cannot be easily reversed. It seems a reasonable course for the FCC to defer consideration of opening the 5.9 GHz band to unlicensed devices until rigorous bench and field testing has proven that 5.9 GHz DSRC systems can be fully protected from harmful interference.

Other Autonomous Vehicle Technology Communications Policy Issues

While the upcoming FCC decision over the spectrum currently used by DSRC has received considerable attention, there are also other important policy issues raised by telematics and communications. In this section, we briefly discuss some of them.

Distracted Driving Laws

Stakeholder interviews identified a wide variety of potential issues concerning communications for AVs. For example, the creation of a communications platform in AVs that can be used for driver assistance and safety reasons may also be used for voice communications, navigation assistance, and infotainment. More than one stakeholder suggested there could be conflicts with states' distracted driving laws and regulations, especially concerning navigation systems. Distracted driving laws vary widely from state to state, and could pose a challenge for development of a standard communications platform for AVs. State lawmakers should begin to consider updating distracted driving laws to accommodate AV technologies.

Developmental Standards

Similarly, another stakeholder explained that the screen size and design of communications platforms within AVs will need to be standardized, at least through "best practice" measures, so developers can address a single platform design instead of many—an important point for developmental cost reasons. In order to reach a mass market, these costs will need to be spread across the largest possible number of AVs. Otherwise, they may inhibit AV deployment. A technology developer explained that the size of the processor used for in-vehicle communications platform has to be fairly large, and automakers' decisions on investments in hardware could be critical. According to several stakeholders, the size and type of processor is a developmental cost issue that could either promote or impede the deployment of AVs to the mass market. One stakeholder noted that OEMs are looking to U.S. DOT to help with such standardization, but "mandate is considered a dirty word."

Data Security

Global technology company stakeholders and global auto industry association stakeholders told us that building robust security protocols across many different automakers' vehicles and different communications platforms is likely to be very challenging technically. Similarly, one of the global technology developers who advocated the need for a secure gateway for communications in AVs discussed using cloud-based systems for security. He noted the need for proper protocol layers and the ability to make the communications solution scalable across hundreds of thousands—possibly even millions—of cars. He acknowledged, however, that AVs would be vulnerable to different types of security attack and said everything that applies to the Internet in terms of security concerns would apply to in-vehicle communications. The security requirements for AV communications may be a potential inhibitor to mass deployment.

Data Ownership and Privacy

Data ownership and privacy are related issues. Numerous stakeholders commented on the high value of data that would be gathered by in-vehicle communications platforms about both the vehicle itself and its driver. For example, insurance companies would be interested in individual driving habits and retailers would be very interested in attracting motorists to their locations. Similarly, law enforcement agencies have considerable interest in using such data.

However, there is no clear property regime for ownership and control of such data. We asked everyone we interviewed their opinion about who owned the data obtained by AVs as they move, gather, and transmit information. Not a single stakeholder was certain of the answer.

Some members of the AV industry are already working on how to anonymize vehicle data and aggregate them so that it does not reveal drivers' personally identifiable information. One stakeholder also identified privacy concerning AV data as an issue that "could derail the business," and needs immediate policy attention. Two stakeholders made a comparison to the information captured by EDRs currently installed in automobiles.

Many stakeholders we interviewed identified policy questions concerning data use and legal issues, such as how long AV data should be maintained and by whom. Corollary issues include whether and how AV data can be disposed of or destroyed, and the legal rights of the vehicle owner to have access to vehicle data. Finally, stakeholders raised the issue of whether data gathered, produced, or transmitted by AVs will be discoverable in legal proceedings. Data ownership and privacy issues related to AV communications remain unsettled and an important policy gap.[10]

Conclusion

In this chapter, we reviewed communications and telematics issues closely related to AV technology. After explaining why telematics is critical to the most probable paths of development of this technology, we reviewed the most important communications technologies. We then reviewed stakeholder concerns and the upcoming decision by the FCC on whether to permit sharing of spectrum currently allocated to DSRC. Stakeholders have described a number of technical and policy issues concerning communications and spectrum use by AVs. These issues have the potential to accelerate or inhibit AV deployment. While the pace of utilization of the spectrum allocated to DSRC has been very slow, it remains a potentially useful technology that may facilitate development of AVs. Further research on distracted driving laws, developmental standards, data ownership, and data security issues would be useful.

---

[10] The questions raised by the data issues here are analogous to concerns expressed about the use of "big data" in other contexts.

CHAPTER SIX

Standards and Regulations and Their Application to Autonomous Vehicle Technologies

In this chapter, we provide an overview of motor-vehicle regulations and standards, and describe the existing regulations and standards for AV technologies. We then provide a general discussion of how and under what circumstances these standards and regulations may need to be developed in the future, drawing on the experiences of air-bag rulemaking in particular.

Government regulations and engineering standards are policy instruments used to address safety, health, environment, and other public concerns. *Regulations* are mandatory requirements developed by policymakers that are specified by law and are enforceable by the government. *Standards*, in contrast, are engineering criteria developed by the technology community that specify how a product should be designed or how it should perform.

By themselves, standards have no authority; an industry or group voluntarily adopts them for consistency, interoperability, and safety. In some scenarios and for some industries, demonstrating that products meet well-accepted industry standards may also provide some liability protection for manufacturers. The Society for Automotive Engineering, now known as SAE International, has developed standards for the comfort, fit, and convenience of seat belts in trucks and buses (SAE, 2007); these particular standards are voluntarily met by manufacturers and are not enforced by government regulations. Standards become enforceable law, however, when they are included as part of a regulation. For example, the Federal Motor Vehicle Safety Standards (FMVSSs) specify performance standards for a wide range of safety components that must be met by law, including that vehicles must meet specific crash test–survivability requirements.

Overview of Regulations for Automobiles

Today, the government regulates virtually every aspect of the automobile with the aim of increasing safety while reducing pollution and gas consumption. The U.S. DOT maintains the FMVSSs, which prescribe an array of safety standards and test procedures, from crash-avoidance components (such as brakes and indicators) to crashworthiness features (such as seat belts and air bags) to post-crash factors (such as the integrity of the fuel system).

At the federal level, NHTSA is the primary regulator. In 1966, Congress enacted the National Traffic and Motor Vehicle Safety Act (U.S. Code, 1966) with the primary purpose of reducing fatalities and accidents from motor vehicle crashes.[1] The safety law gives NHTSA authority over "motor vehicles" and "motor vehicle equipment," stating that (U.S. Code, 1966, §30102):

> motor vehicle equipment means—
> (A) any system, part, or component of a motor vehicle as originally manufactured;
> (B) any similar part or component manufactured or sold for replacement or improvement of a system, part or component, or as an accessory or addition to a motor vehicle; or
> (C) any device or an article of apparel, including a motorcycle helmet and excluding medicine or eyeglasses prescribed by a licensed practitioner, that—
> (i) is not a system, part, or component of a motor vehicle; and
> (ii) is manufactured, sold, delivered or offered to be sold for use on public streets, roads and highways with the

---

[1] For a fascinating account of the political history that led to the passage of the 1966 law, see Mashaw and Harfst (1990).

> apparent purpose of safeguarding users of motor vehicles against risk of accident, injury or death.

This is a relatively broad definition of NHTSA's regulatory authority and would certainly encompass most (both OEM and aftermarket) AV technology.[2]

The 1966 law provides NHTSA with several tools. First, it can create FMVSSs, and automakers must certify that their cars meet the relevant standards in place at the time of manufacture. For example, FMVSS No. 208 (1999) governs the specific performance criteria that must be met by air bags. These standards must be performance-oriented, "practicable," "objective," and "meet the need for safety."[3]

Second, if a manufacturer's product fails to comply with an applicable FMVSS, or contains an unreasonable risk to motor vehicle safety, the manufacturer must recall the vehicle and remedy the problem. While NHTSA has the authority to require a recall, typically the manufacturer initiates one voluntarily, often following an investigation by NHTSA (Wood et al., 2012). The ability to order a recall in the case of a defect offers NHTSA another means to regulate AVs should safety problems that can be traced to a defect arise.

Third, NHTSA can indirectly influence the marketplace by its New Car Assessment Program. Through this program, NHTSA evaluates the safety of cars and provides a rating from one to five stars based on their performance in crash-testing and roll-over resistance tests. In turn, manufacturers often use these ratings in advertising their cars. More recently, in evaluating cars, NHTSA has noted the presence or absence of crash avoidance systems: electronic stability control, lane departure warning, and forward collision warning. The manufacturer must meet NHTSA's standards for its product to be included in the list of cars that include such devices.

---

[2]   For a thorough exploration of NHTSA's authority, see Wood et al. (2012).

[3]   The U.S. Code defines "motor vehicle safety standard" as "a minimum standard for motor vehicle or motor vehicle equipment performance" (U.S. Code, 1966, §30102(a)(9); §30111(a)).

It is also important to note the limitations on NHTSA's authority. It does not directly regulate the operation of cars, the actions of vehicle owners, maintenance, or repair. NHTSA also has no authority over modifications that vehicle owners may make on their own. It can, however, prohibit third-party modifications of vehicles in ways that interfere with safety. More precisely, the transportation law prohibits businesses from "mak[ing] inoperative any part of a device or element of design installed on or in a motor vehicle or motor vehicle equipment in compliance with an applicable [FMVSS]" (U.S. Code, 2006). Except with respect to commercial vehicles, NHTSA also cannot require retrofitting existing vehicles with new equipment (U.S. Code of Federal Regulations, 2010).[4] NHTSA must therefore rely on states to conduct periodic (often annual) inspections of motor vehicles to ensure that they are safe and roadworthy (although not all states choose to do so). To that end, NHTSA has created safety standards that can be used by the states to conduct inspections.[5]

Case Study: Air-Bag Regulation

Like many AV technologies, the automatic intervention of air bags in a crash shifts safety responsibilities (such as using active restraints) from the drivers and other vehicle occupants to the vehicle and its manufacturer. In doing so, it also reflects a shift in liability from the driver to the manufacturer. Thus, experiences with air-bag regulation are particularly relevant to AV technologies. Here, we provide a brief history of air bags as a case study of rulemaking for emerging safety technologies. Later, we discuss their implications for AV technology standards and regulation.

Air bags were initially introduced in the early 1970s in higher-end models (Mackay, 1991). At that time, they were marketed as alternatives to seat belts, rather than as supplements. Jameson M. Wetmore

---

[4] The U.S. Code of Federal Regulations (2010) provides NHTSA with authority to promulgate safety standards for commercial motor vehicles after manufacture of vehicle.

[5] U.S. Code of Federal Regulations (2010), pt. 570.

(2004, p. 390) notes the perspective of policymakers and industry experts at the time:

> They argued that a system of inflatable pillows could be automatically deployed inside a vehicle in the event of a collision that would hold occupants in place even if they were not wearing seat belts. They contended that such a system would replace both seat belts and the need to rely on automobile occupants to engage a restraint device.

In that era, voluntary seat-belt usage was quite low. Using the logic that air bags would make seat belts unnecessary, NHTSA initiated efforts in the 1970s to pass regulations requiring air bags in all U.S. automobiles. Such regulations met with significant resistance from most automobile manufacturers, which did not want either the responsibility or the liability for the losses resulting from crashes and did not believe these safety features would sell. This tension produced "a standoff between air-bag proponents and the automakers that resulted in contentious debates, several court cases, and very few air bags" (Wetmore, 2004, p. 391).

In 1984, the U.S. DOT passed a ruling requiring vehicles manufactured after 1990 to be equipped with some type of passive restraint system; e.g., air bags or automatic seat belts (Wetmore, 2004). In 1991, this regulation was amended to require air bags in particular in all automobiles by 1999 (Public Law 102-240). The mandatory performance standards in the FMVSSs further required air bags to protect an unbelted adult male passenger in a head-on, 30-mph crash. Additionally, by 1990, the situation had changed dramatically, and air bags were being installed in millions of cars. Wetmore attributes this development to three factors: First, technology had advanced to enable air-bag deployment with high reliability; second, public attitude shifted and safety features became important factors for consumers; and, third, air bags were no longer being promoted as replacements but as *supplements* to seat belts, which resulted in a sharing of responsibility between manufacturers and passengers and lessened manufacturers' potential liability (Wetmore, 2004).

While air bags have certainly saved many lives, they have not lived up to original expectations: In 1977, NHTSA estimated that air bags would save on the order of 9,000 lives per year and based its regulations on these expectations (Thompson, Segui-Gomez, and Graham, 2002). Today, by contrast, NHTSA calculates that air bags saved a total of 8,369 lives in the 14 years between 1987 and 2001 (Glassbrenner, undated). Simultaneously, however, it became evident that first-generation air bags posed a risk to many passengers, particularly smaller passengers, such as women of small stature, the elderly, and children. NHTSA (2008a) determined that 291 deaths were caused by air bags between 1990 and July 2008, primarily due to the extreme force that is necessary to meet the performance standard of protecting the unbelted adult male passenger. Houston and Richardson (2000) describe the strong reaction to these losses and a backlash against air bags, despite their benefits.

The unintended consequences of air bags have led to technology developments and changes to standards and regulations. Between 1997 and 2000, NHTSA developed a number of interim solutions designed to reduce the risks of air bags, including on-off switches and deployment with less force (Ho, 2006). Simultaneously, safer air bags were developed that deploy with a force tailored to the occupant by taking into account the seat position, belt usage, occupant weight, and other factors. In 2000, NHTSA mandated that the introduction of these advanced air bags begin in 2003 and that, by 2006, every new passenger vehicle would include these safety measures (NHTSA, 2000).

What lessons does this experience offer for regulation of AV technologies? We suggest that modest expectations and flexibility are necessary. The early air-bag regulators envisioned air bags as being a substitute for seat belts because the rates of belt usage were so low and appeared intractable. Few anticipated that usage of seat belts would rise as much as it has and that air bags would eventually be used more as a supplement than a substitute for seat belts. Similarly unexpected developments are likely to arise in the context of AV technologies.

The air bag experience is also instructive, perhaps depressingly so, because there was a long lag between the time that the technology was developed and the time it was actually widespread. The first air-bag patents were issued in the early 1950s; by the early 1970s, air-bag manufacturing companies existed and the technology was reasonably mature (Mashaw and Harfst, 1990). Yet they were in very few cars and it was not until 1999, nearly 20 years later, that air bags were ultimately required in all cars. Thousands of car crash fatalities might have been prevented by air bags in the interim. Developing the technology was a necessary but not sufficient condition for the technology to be used.

Current Standards and Regulations for Autonomous Vehicle Technologies

The need for both standards and regulations for some of these AV technologies has been recognized. In 2001, the NTSB issued a report analyzing ACC and CWSs and emphasized the importance of both performance standards and regulations. The NTSB recommended that the U.S. DOT complete rulemaking on performance standards for both technologies in both commercial and passenger vehicles and that the agency also require installation of CWSs in all commercial vehicles. Without standards for system operation and driver interaction, the NTSB felt that the use of a variety of systems would lead to driver confusion and incorrect interventions and responses to system behavior (NTSB, 2001).

There are currently no federal regulations related specifically to AV technologies, though both NHTSA and RITA are examining the issue. None of these technologies is, to date, required in any type of vehicle, and there are no mandatory standards related to their specific design or performance. As suggested by the experiences of air-bag regulation, there are likely to be several closely related reasons for this. First, regulatory promulgation is fundamentally an iterative and slow process, given the cycles of proposals, requests for comments, reviews, and lobbying that precede rulemaking. Second, with AV technologies in particular, their newness and rapid evolution create uncertainty in both rulemaking effects and of the technology itself.

Moreover, with rapid technology changes, it can be challenging to prescribe rules that will remain relevant and appropriate through the development process (van Wees, 2004). A government transportation official we interviewed stated that, when it came to issuing standards, he thought it was extremely difficult to stay relevant, given the swift pace of technological change.

Third, reaching a consensus is difficult, given the many stakeholders (manufacturers, government, nongovernmental organizations and private citizens). For example, NHTSA's New Car Assessment Program includes a rating system indicating whether advanced safety technologies, such as forward CWSs, are available in a particular car model. However, this rating system does not evaluate or differentiate among technologies, in part because of significant differences and disagreement among manufacturers and consumer groups as to whether and how these technologies ought to be evaluated (NHTSA, 2008b). Fourth, industry is generally resistant to regulation, often citing price increases that the market may not necessarily bear, undesirable constraints on design and development, and superior alternatives to government regulation, such as industry-developed standards and rules. An AV developer we interviewed identified regulation as a "big concern." He noted that technology does not always evolve in expected directions, which can render regulations and standards obsolete, or worse, a barrier to development.

Although regulatory promulgation has yet to occur, there are numerous national and international government and industry efforts to develop principles, guidelines, and standards for AV technologies. The Crash Avoidance Metrics Partnership brings auto manufacturers together on projects that "accelerate the implementation of crash avoidance countermeasures to improve traffic safety by defining and developing necessary pre-competitive enabling elements of future systems" (Shulman and Deering, 2005, p. 3). It includes, for example, the Forward Collision Warning Requirements Project, which addresses alert function and interface requirements through real and simulated tests with human drivers. Several organizations address intelligent transport systems more broadly. The International Harmonized Research Activities Working Group on Intelligent Transport Systems (IHRA-ITS) was put together to lead research and encourage collaboration on related safety issues; one of the objectives is to conduct research that provides a strong grounding for internationally harmonized regulations (Burns, 2013; IHRA-ITS, 2008). The International Organization for Standardization (ISO) has set up an international working group (ISO/TC204/

WG14) under its intelligent transport systems technical committee to evaluate design guidelines and recommend standards for any technologies that aid in "avoiding crashes; increasing roadway efficiency; adding to driver convenience; reducing driver workload; improving the level of travellers' safety, security, and assistance . . . warn of impending danger; advise of corrective actions; partially or fully automate driving tasks; report travellers' distress; and request needed emergency services" (APEC, 2006). The SAE similarly has an intelligent transport systems division that addresses these technologies.

Such organizational and research efforts have been fruitful. The U.S. DOT has published a set of voluntary operational requirements for CWSs and ACC (Houser, Pierowicz, and McClellan, 2005), but it does not serve as a standard, specification, or regulation. The ISO and SAE have published several standards related to AV technologies.[6] Other related standards are discussed by the IHRA-ITS (2008).

These standards are just beginning to be articulated, no doubt in part because these technologies are themselves under development. First, the standards are not yet precisely defined. For example, the ISO standard for lane departure warning states, "An easily perceivable haptic and/or audible warning shall be provided" (ISO, 2007a). But, what does "easily perceivable" mean and for what population of drivers? Similarly, the SAE standard for ACC includes specifications for sensors: "ACC systems shall be capable of responding to all licensable motorized road vehicles, including motorcycles, intended for use on public roads" (SAE, 2003b). Yet, this does not specify the environmental conditions under which this is to hold true. Additionally, although these standards include many specifications and some basic test procedures, essentially nothing has been written with the primary

---

[6] E.g., SAE's *Adaptive Cruise Control (ACC) Operating Characteristics and User Interface* (2003a); SAE's *Human Factors in Forward Collision Warning Systems: Operating Characteristics and User Interface Requirements* (2003b); ISO, *Transport Information and Control Systems: Adaptive Cruise Control Systems: Performance Requirements and Test Procedures* (2007b); ISO, *Transport Information and Control Systems: Forward Vehicle Collision Warning Systems: Performance Requirements and Test Procedures* (2008a); ISO, *Intelligent Transport Systems: Lane Departure Warning System: Performance Requirements and Test Procedures* (2007a); ISO, *Intelligent Transport Systems: Lane Change Decision Aid Systems (LCDAS): Performance Requirements and Test Procedures* (2008b).

objective of defining conformance requirements (i.e., test methods and procedures). Such conformance requirements are necessary to determine whether a technology or system is actually in compliance with the specifications (APEC, 2006). Moreover, where test procedures are described, the environmental conditions are either ideal or unspecified.

On the other hand, a global technology company executive we interviewed thought an ISO standard concerning "Functional Risks" (ISO 26262 for automobiles) was important to reduce liability. He said if auto manufacturers adhere to ISO standards, they can argue that they are operating at the state of the art or industry and have observed mechanisms for functional safety. He said this was a key area for development, stating that standards (such as new ISO specifications) and best practices go hand in hand to reduce liability.

Future Implications for Standards and Regulations for Autonomous Vehicle Technologies

We now outline some of the issues that policymakers should address for standards and regulations for AV technologies. These observations are necessarily somewhat speculative, given the numerous uncertainties involved.

Standards and Regulations to Facilitate Human-Machine Interaction

AV technologies, like air bags, will be used by a wide range of drivers and passengers. Recall that standards for air bags were set for only a limited section of the driver and passenger population—namely, average male adults. It became apparent only after widespread implementation that they put smaller passengers at risk of injury or death. AV technologies, too, will affect different people differently. In the case of driver-warning systems, for example, users' expectations of how and when the technology will work and their ability to understand the system's directions and warnings will affect the effectiveness of the technology. Therefore, standards must be developed that take into account diverse populations and varying expectations. Simultaneously, drivers are also likely to use AV technologies in vehicles developed by different manufacturers.

As we have discussed, driver interaction and involvement is critical to many AV technologies (e.g., warning systems that operate specifically by influencing the driver, and other technologies, such as ACC, that must be activated by the driver and require the driver to intervene at critical moments). As the NTSB has suggested, standardizing these technologies will be particularly important to achieving safety goals.

Regulations may also help coordinate expectations. Suppose pedestrians become accustomed to cars automatically braking in their presence. Regulation of these functions will help minimize hazards that may arise if pedestrian expectations and cars' capacities are not aligned.

Performance Standards and Regulations

The significant difference between traditional automotive technologies and AV technologies is that AV technologies sense and make judgments about the vehicle's external environment, which cannot be controlled and can vary tremendously in terms of other vehicular traffic on the road, pedestrians and other road users, static objects, the quality of road itself and road elements (e.g., lane markings and signs), and weather and lighting conditions. Therefore, the performance requirements of sensors and sensor-fusion systems that build the vehicle's world model are extremely important. As discussed, a variety of sensors can be employed for each type of AV technology, many sensors are likely to be employed in concert, and each type of sensor has different operating specifications and may not operate effectively in some environments. Given this, it seems clear that performance standards for AV technologies must specify the environmental conditions under which the tests must occur and, ideally, will include testing under a wide range of environmental conditions.

For technologies at one end of the spectrum (e.g., Levels 0, 1, and 2) that leave the driver in at least some control of the vehicle at all times (e.g., driver-warning systems and ACC), conformance requirements that specify a smaller set of environmental conditions may be acceptable as the driver is ultimately still responsible for interpreting the environment and determining whether these technologies ought to be used. However, as we move toward vehicles that are fully autonomous and driverless, the standards and testing need to span the *entire* range of conditions in which the vehicle might be expected to operate. Anticipating and testing operation under all possible scenarios is extremely challenging and likely to be a significant barrier to deploying AVs absent additional operational experience with these technologies. Given these obstacles, it is also possible that future policies and technologies will try to control the environment of AVs (for example, by segregating lanes strictly for AVs or limiting their operation to certain areas or conditions).[7]

Conclusion

Mandating the inclusion of AV technologies may not be appropriate until at least the following circumstances are met. First, the technology must be mature enough that manufacturers are confident in their operation or are confident that they will not be held liable if they do not operate perfectly. This might require modifications to the liability regime (as discussed in the next chapter). In the 1970s, when air-bag regulations were initially being developed, manufacturers were not confident in the sensing capabilities of air bag–deployment sensors and, partly for this reason, resisted the mandate to include air bags. Despite the fact that even partially effective air bags could save many lives, they feared liability for the cases in which the air bags did not properly deploy (Mashaw and Harfst, 1990). A similar policy standoff could occur between lawmakers and manufacturers if regulatory requirements for AV technologies appear to place a greater liability burden on manufacturers.

Second, the safety effects ought to be well understood. Certainly, this includes understanding the performance of different technologies in different conditions and with different users. This research baseline does not yet exist.

Third, the costs and benefits need to be accurately assessed. We now know that the benefits of air bags were significantly overestimated at the time of rulemaking and that the actual benefits, while substantial, were fewer, resulting in criticism of air bags overall as a safety mea-

---

[7] Existing dedicated busways may prove to be relatively controlled environments in which to pilot these efforts.

sure. Similarly, many expect AV technology to dramatically improve safety and reduce the incidence and effects of crashes. While initial evidence supports the benefits of these technologies, accurate estimates of costs and benefits are critical for policymakers to develop appropriate rules and for manufacturers, insurance companies, consumers, and other stakeholders to make appropriate decisions. While Chapter Two does cover some rough estimates of the likely costs and benefits, more detailed estimates can be developed by using existing data on the costs of conventional driving and specific assumptions based on the state of the art of AV technology.

CHAPTER SEVEN

Liability Implications of Autonomous Vehicle Technology

In Chapter Two, we discussed the advantages of this technology and rough estimates of its short- and long-term implications. While there are considerable uncertainties involved with any new technology, we concluded that there was substantial potential for this technology to improve social welfare. This chapter focuses on the operation of tort liability laws in the United States and its risks to the development of this technology. Gary Marchant and Rachel Lindor (2012, p. 1334) outlined one such scenario: [1]

> The technology is potentially doomed if there are a significant number of . . . cases, because the liability burden on the manufacturer may be prohibitive of further development. Thus, even though an autonomous vehicle may be safer overall than a conventional vehicle, it will shift the responsibility for accidents, and hence liability, from drivers to manufacturers. The shift will push the manufacturer away from the socially optimal outcome—to develop the autonomous vehicle.

This chapter reviews the liability implications of AV technology and discusses possible solutions. We first discuss tort liability for drivers and insurers and then discuss manufacturer liability. [2]

---

[1] For similar predictions, see also Kalra, Anderson, and Wachs (2009) and Ayers (1994).

[2] Because most current efforts are focused on developing AVs that do not depend on specialized infrastructure, we do not discuss the liability implications of "intelligent" infrastructure. In general, state and federal governments will be shielded by the doctrine of sovereign immunity, though this will not shield municipalities or private contractors—and even as to

Tort Liability for Drivers and Insurers

The law governing crashes is a mixture of state tort law and state financial responsibility laws that mandate insurance for drivers. As a result, the mandatory-insurance regime substantially affects litigation that occurs after crashes. We begin by discussing driver liability and then apply these theories of liability to AV technologies.

Theories of Driver Liability

There are three basic theories of tort liability that affect drivers—traditional negligence, no-fault liability, and strict liability—and we discuss each in turn.[3]

Under traditional negligence principles, people are civilly liable for harms they cause if the harm is a tort. The wrongdoer (*tortfeasor*) must compensate the victim for the harms suffered.[4] The traditional elements of a negligent tort are the existence of a duty, the breach of that duty, causation, and injury. In the case of automobiles, drivers have a duty to take reasonable care in operation. Drivers are liable for injuries that they cause in violation of this duty of reasonable care.

The central idea of liability for negligence is that a party should be held liable for harms caused by *unreasonably* failing to prevent the risk. For example, suppose a man drives a car with defective brakes because he is too lazy to get the brakes repaired. As a result of his defective brakes, he injures a pedestrian. In this hypothetical, the man will probably be found negligent. It was not *reasonable* for him to fail to repair his brakes.

---

the state and federal government, important exceptions apply. More research on this complex issue and its implications would be useful.

[3] *Tort* is a general term for wrong and is also a term that refers to the general legal field of torts. A *negligent tort* is a particular category of tort. Other categories include *intentional tort* (the wrongdoer deliberately harms the victim) and *strict-liability torts* (the wrongdoer is liable for harms regardless of whether he or she took reasonable care to prevent them).

[4] In some cases, the tortfeasor must pay punitive damages in addition to those necessary to compensate the victim (*compensatory damages*).

For good and bad, *reasonableness* is a fairly vague concept.[5] In the day-to-day resolution of automobile crash claims, the operation of the traditional system of liability for negligence has been influenced by the mandatory-insurance system. Insurance adjusters have adopted informal rules to effectively allocate fault (e.g., drivers who rear-end other vehicles are presumed to be at fault). These have minimized more-general analyses of reasonableness and causation in most automobile crash cases, which are resolved without formal litigation. So rather than undertaking a generalized analysis of whether a driver is negligent and therefore liable for a crash—a potentially difficult and open-ended inquiry—an insurance adjuster is likely to refer to a simpler set of rules to determine who owes what to whom (Hensler et al., 1991; Ross, 1980, p. 237: "The law of negligence was made to lean heavily upon the much simpler traffic law").

Twelve states use an alternative system, called *no-fault*, for automobile-crash litigation and insurance. In these states, automobile crash victims are not permitted to sue other drivers in the tort system unless their injuries reach a certain degree of severity, called a *threshold*.[6] Instead, victims are directly compensated for their losses through their own insurance. Proponents of this system argued that it would eliminate the difficult determination of who, if anyone, was at fault for a particular crash, ensure that compensation would be available to victims regardless of whether anyone was legally at fault, and generally reduce litigation and lawsuits.[7]

---

[5] Anderson (2007) argues that economic analysis of tort law is indeterminate without a theory of which variables should be in the cost-benefit calculus.

[6] States have adopted either a monetary or verbal threshold. A *monetary threshold* is a certain dollar amount that the victim's injuries have to exceed to recover in tort ($5,000 in many states). A *verbal threshold* is a description of a certain degree of seriousness. In Pennsylvania, for example, a plaintiff who elects the limitation on tort when purchasing automobile insurance must show that his or her injury is "serious" to recover in tort (Pennsylvania Statutes, Title 75, §1705). "Serious" is defined as "a personal injury resulting in death, serious impairment of body function or permanent serious disfigurement" (Pennsylvania Statutes, Title 75, §1702).

[7] It has proven somewhat disappointing in practice, with costs remaining higher than expected. See Anderson, Heaton, and Carroll (2010).

A rare theory of liability that might also affect operators of AV technologies is strict liability for abnormally dangerous or "ultrahazardous" activities. The rationale for this type of liability is that actors involved in highly unusual activities are more knowledgeable about the risks that such activity entails and should consequently bear the associated costs regardless of whether they are legally at fault for the crash.[8] This theory of liability may be particularly relevant to liability of drivers of early AVs. Victims of AV-related crashes may sue the owners or drivers of the vehicles and argue that the operation of AV technologies constituted an ultrahazardous activity and the operators should therefore be strictly liable for any crashes that occur, regardless of whether they were negligent. Graham (2012) makes a similar observation when noting the liability of early adopters of new technologies.

Autonomous Vehicle Technologies, Liability of Drivers, and Insurance

How will AV technologies affect driver liability for automobile crashes? First, these technologies will likely reduce the number and overall cost of crashes for the reasons discussed in Chapter Two. Human error causes the vast majority of crashes today, and, by reducing the risk of human error, AV technologies can reduce the incidence of crashes. This will, in turn, likely reduce automobile-insurance costs. To encourage adoption, insurers may offer discounts for operators who purchase automobiles with the appropriate systems. Historically, insurance companies have been important intermediaries in recognizing the safety benefits of technologies that reduce risk and encouraging their policy-

---

[8]   This theory of liability is set forth in §§519–524A of the *Restatement of the Law, Second: Torts* (ALI, 1977): "One who carries on an abnormally dangerous activity is subject to liability for harm to the person, land or chattels of another resulting from the activity, although he has exercised the utmost care to prevent the harm." §520 sets forth the following factors to be considered in determining whether an activity is abnormally dangerous or ultrahazardous:

> (a) existence of a high degree of risk of some harm to the person, land or chattels of others; (b) likelihood that the harm that results from it will be great; (c) inability to eliminate the risk by the exercise of reasonable care; (d) extent to which the activity is not a matter of common usage; (e) inappropriateness of the activity to the place where it is carried on; and (f) extent to which its value to the community is outweighed by its dangerous attributes.

holders to invest in them. In Europe, for example, insurers have offered a 20-percent discount on automobile insurance for policyholders who purchase a car with a lane keeping function and ACC.[9]

If these technologies reduce crashes sufficiently, it is possible that the very need for specialized automobile insurance may disappear entirely. Injuries that result from automobile crashes might be covered by health insurance and homeowner's liability insurance, in the way that bicycle crashes or other crashes are now covered. It is not clear how much crashes would have to be reduced to make specialized automobile-accident insurance undesirable. In theory, automobile-accident costs could today be covered under other policies, though this would require a substantial revision of state law and insurance markets and is probably unlikely in the near term.

Second, AV technologies may undermine the degree to which a driver must necessarily be at fault for a crash. Currently, the driver is generally considered exclusively responsible for control of the vehicle. Hence, we commonly speak of crashes as being *caused* by one or more at-fault drivers. In the vast majority of crashes, we ascribe blame to one or more drivers rather than to design features of the car.[10] AV technologies will likely dilute the sense that drivers are directly and solely responsible for their automobiles. By shifting responsibility for the automobile from the human driver to the car or its manufacturer, these systems are likely to undermine the conventional social attribution of blame for automobile crashes.[11]

This reduction in fault may be roughly proportional to the extent to which the particular technology apparently controls the car. As

---

[9] It is unclear whether the discount is partially subsidized by the automobile manufacturer (see Loh, 2008).

[10] In theory, injuries suffered in crashes could be said to be caused by the manufacturer's design decision to allow automobiles to exceed 20 mph instead of blaming crashes on (inevitable) driver error. The attribution of responsibility or causation for a crash (or any event) is a complex process and there are a variety of plausible candidates. Choosing one has policy implications. See Calabresi (1975, p. 73).

[11] Automobile manufacturers resisted air bags in part for this reason: concern that legal responsibility for crashes would shift from the driver to manufacturers (Wetmore, 2004, p. 391).

explained in Chapter One, the technology operates on a continuum between complete driver control and complete automobile control. If the technology simply provides additional information to the driver (e.g., lane departure warning), it is less likely to undermine the sense to which the driver retains ultimate responsibility for the vehicle. In contrast, if a car with an engaged autopilot feature crashes into a car in front of it and the driver's use of the autopilot was proper, it seems odd to argue that the driver was at fault.[12] In crashes that involve drivers reasonably relying on a car's ability to control itself, there may not be an at-fault driver for the victim to sue.

This shift in responsibility from the driver to the manufacturer may make no-fault automobile-insurance regimes more attractive. While the victims in these circumstances could presumably sue the vehicle manufacturer, product-liability lawsuits are more expensive to bring and typically take more time to resolve than run-of-the-mill automobile-crash litigation. No-fault systems are designed to provide compensation to victims relatively quickly, and they do not depend upon the identification of an "at-fault" party.

Third, this technology may also change the distribution of harms caused by crashes, which may have insurance consequences. Presently, the vast majority of crashes result in relatively minor harm, and these minor crashes vastly outnumber the major ones. Suppose that AV technologies are remarkably effective at virtually eliminating minor crashes caused by human error. It may be that the comparatively few crashes that do still occur usually result in very serious injuries or fatalities (e.g., because the vehicles are operating at much higher speeds or densities). Or, perhaps, if a crash is the result of a programming error, the error might simultaneously affect many cars at once.

---

[12] As tort scholars have long recognized, the assignment of legal responsibility (and liability) does not, in theory, need to match our sense of moral responsibility (see Calabresi and Hirschoff, 1972, arguing that liability could be placed on the cheapest-cost avoider—the party that is in the position to avoid the costs most cheaply). For example, one could hold automobile operators strictly liable for crashes that resulted from the operation of their automobiles, regardless of fault (defined either morally or economically). More recently, corrective-justice and civil-recourse tort theorists have questioned whether disconnecting legal responsibility from the sense of wrong is consistent with many features of tort law. See, e.g., Coleman (1992).

This kind of change in the distribution of crashes may affect the economics of insuring against them. Actuarially, it is much easier for an insurance company to calculate the expected costs of somewhat common small crashes than the costs of rarer, much larger events. This may limit the downward trend in automobile-insurance costs that we would otherwise expect and make insuring against auto crashes more complex.[13]

Further, new categories of crashes might arise, and these might pose interesting questions of how the liability system sets incentives to coordinate care among parties. For example, suppose that most cars brake automatically when they sense a pedestrian in their path. As more cars with this feature come to be on the road, pedestrians may expect that cars will stop, in the same way that people stick their limbs in elevator doors confident that the door will automatically reopen. The general level of pedestrian care may decline as people become accustomed to this common safety feature. But if there were a few models of cars that did not stop in the same way, a new category of crashes could emerge. In this case, should pedestrians be able to recover damages if they are injured after wrongly assuming a car would automatically stop? To allow recovery in this instance would seem to undermine incentives for pedestrians to take efficient care. On the other hand, allowing damages to the injured pedestrian may encourage the universal adoption of this safety feature. Since negligence is defined by unreasonableness, the evolving set of shared assumptions about the operation of the roadways—what counts as "reasonable"—will determine liability.

Fourth, we think that it is not likely that operators of vehicles that are partially or fully autonomous will be found strictly liable with driving such vehicles as an ultrahazardous activity. As explained earlier, these technologies will likely be introduced incrementally and will initially serve merely to aid the driver rather than take full control of the vehicle. This will give the public and courts time to become familiar with the capabilities and limits of the technology. As a result, it seems

---

[13] Auto insurers may also be hampered from offering discounts for the use of AV technology by the fact that automobile insurance is regulated at the state level and state regulations about insurance pricing vary widely.

unlikely that courts will consider its gradual introduction and use to be ultrahazardous. On the other hand, this would not be true if a person attempted to operate a car fully autonomously before the technology adequately matured. If, for example, a home hobbyist put together his own AV and attempted to operate it on public roads, victims of any crashes that resulted may well be successful in convincing a court to find the operator strictly liable on the grounds that such activity was ultrahazardous.

Overall, we do not anticipate that liability for individual drivers will be a problematic obstacle or deterrent to the use of AV technologies. On the contrary, the decrease in the expected probability of a crash and associated lower insurance costs that AV technologies will bring about will probably encourage adoption of these technologies by drivers and automobile-insurance companies. As responsibility for crashes shifts away from the driver, no-fault systems may become more attractive.

On the other hand, these technologies pose challenges for manufacturers and may increase their liability risk in ways that may discourage the efficient introduction of these technologies.

Liability of Manufacturers

Current liability laws may well lead to inefficient delays in manufacturers introducing AV technologies. The gradual shift in responsibility for automobile operation from the driver to the vehicle may lead to a similar shift in liability for crashes from the driver to the manufacturer. Recognizing this effect, manufacturers may be reluctant to introduce technology that will increase their liability. Alternatively, manufacturers may price this technology to recover their expected liability costs. This may lead to higher prices and lower adoption of this technology than would be socially optimal.

Liability of automobile manufacturers is governed by product-liability law, which is a hybrid of tort and contract law concerned with the liability of manufacturers for their products. Substantial variations exist among states, but many states have adopted portions of the

American Law Institute's (ALI's) *Restatement of the Law, Second: Torts* (ALI, 1977) and *Restatement of the Law, Third: Torts—Products Liability* (ALI, 1998). These restatements are efforts to systematize the law. While not automatically binding on any court, many state supreme courts adopt portions of the restatements to govern particular areas of the law.[14]

The Role of Cost-Benefit Analysis

Negligence is the most common theory of liability and is the legal standard most often used in tort law. As explained earlier, the central idea of liability for negligence is that a party should be held liable for harms it caused by its *unreasonable* failure to prevent the risk. While equating negligence with cost-benefit analysis has been criticized by many theorists as reductive and eliminating the subtleties of negligence (see, e.g., Vandall, 1986), some form of cost-benefit analysis remains influential in product-liability cases. Recently, courts and the restatement reporters have been reintroducing the core concept of negligence—reasonableness (and, in some cases, cost-benefit analysis)—into other theories of product liability.

While it is difficult to generalize, automobile (and subsystem) manufacturers may fare well under a legal standard that uses a cost-benefit analysis that includes crashes avoided from the use of AV technologies. Under such a regime, automakers could argue that the overall benefits from the use of a particular technology outweigh the risks, as discussed in Chapter Two. The number of crashes avoided by the use of these technologies is likely to be large.

In contrast, plaintiffs will likely seek to exclude any global cost-benefit analysis that considers the benefits of avoided crashes and try to focus the reasonableness analysis on the specific facts around the crash (for example, was the automobile manufacturer reasonable in failing to include a warning about sleeping while the ACC and lane keeping functions were engaged? What were the costs and benefits of that par-

---

[14] A comprehensive exploration of the theories of liability and kinds of defect that might be used by injured parties is beyond the scope of this paper. We refer interested readers to Marchant and Lindor (2012), Gurney (2013), and Kalra, Anderson, and Wachs (2009).

ticular decision?). The plaintiff would likely argue that evidence about the numerous crashes prevented by this technology was irrelevant. By focusing on the specific circumstances of the particular crash, plaintiffs will attempt to focus the reasonableness and cost-benefit analysis away from the long-term safety benefits of these technologies.

Unfortunately, the socially optimal liability rule is often unclear. Permitting the defendant to include the long-run benefits in the cost-benefit analysis may encourage the adoption of technology that can save many lives. On the other hand, it may shield the manufacturer from liability for shorter-run decisions that were inefficiently dangerous. Suppose, for example, that a crash-prevention system operates successfully 70 percent of the time but that, with additional time and work, it could have been designed to operate successfully 90 percent of the time. Then suppose that a victim is injured in a crash that would have been prevented had the system worked 90 percent of the time. Assume that the adoption of the 70-percent technology is socially desirable but the adoption of the 90-percent technology would be even more socially desirable. How should the cost-benefit analysis be conducted? Is the manufacturer permitted to cite the 70 percent of crashes that were prevented in arguing for the benefits of the technology? Or should the cost-benefit analysis focus on the manufacturer's failure to design the product to function at 90-percent effectiveness? If the latter, the manufacturer might not employ the technology at all, thereby leading to many preventable crashes. In calculating the marginal cost of the 90-percent technology, should the manufacturer be able to count the lives lost in the delay in implementation as compared to possible release of the 70-percent technology? A host of important definitional issues as to what can be counted as cost and benefit must first be resolved. These issues make the integration of cost-benefit analysis into tort law complex.[15]

Strict product liability. Strict product liability is an alternative theory of liability available to victims in lieu of having to prove negligence. Strict liability is conventionally contrasted with negligence because, in theory, it does not require any showing of negligence,

---

[15] See Anderson (2007) for discussion of these issues.

unreasonableness, or any kind of fault on the part of the defendant. In its most extreme interpretation, strict product liability means that manufacturers insure users against all harms that come from their product, regardless of fault. Proponents of this loss-spreading rationale argue that strict liability can and should serve this compensation function and that manufacturers could easily pass on the additional costs of tort judgments to consumers by raising the prices of their products (see Priest and Owen, 1985). Manufacturers would also have the appropriate incentives to reduce the danger of their products. While this expansive version of strict liability has not been adopted, the rationale of broad liability to spread costs underlies strict tort liability as it actually functions today.[16]

In most states, strict tort liability is governed by §402A in ALI (1977).[17] Under §402A, the seller of a product is liable for harm caused by such product when it is sold in a "defective condition unreasonably dangerous to the user." A product is deemed defective if it "left the supplier's control lacking any element necessary to make it safe for its intended use or possessing any feature that renders it unsafe for the intended use" (ALI, 1977). Under §402A, the imposition of strict liability for a product defect is not affected by the fact that the manufacturer

---

[16] Every state except Delaware, Massachusetts, Michigan, North Carolina, and Virginia has adopted strict liability in tort of some form. The states that have rejected strict liability in tort often achieve similar ends through interpretation of warranty law (Owen, Montgomery, and Davis, 2007, §5.3).

[17] ALI (1977) §402A, "Special Liability of Seller of Product for Physical Harm to User or Consumer," states:

> One who sells any product in a defective condition unreasonably dangerous to the user or consumer or to his property is subject to liability for physical harm thereby caused to the ultimate user or consumer, or to his property, if (a) the seller is engaged in the business of selling such a product, and (b) it is expected to and does reach the user or consumer without substantial change in the condition in which it is sold. (2) The rule stated in Subsection (1) applies although (a) the seller has exercised all possible care in the preparation and sale of his product, and (b) the user or consumer has not bought the product from or entered into any contractual relation with the seller. Caveat: The Institute expresses no opinion as to whether the rules stated in this Section may not apply (1) to harm to persons other than users or consumers; (2) to the seller of a product expected to be processed or otherwise substantially changed before it reaches the user or consumer; or (3) to the seller of a component part of a product to be assembled.

or other supplier has exercised all possible care. However, litigation about whether a product is *unreasonably* dangerous often introduces an analysis of the reasonableness of the manufacturers' actions—a study that usually resembles the analysis of reasonableness that occurs in negligence cases, and can include the same cost-benefit issues that were discussed earlier.

Some states have adopted §2 of ALI (1998). Published approximately 30 years after §402A first appeared, it incorporates some of the relevant jurisprudence that has developed as courts have interpreted §402A. It retains the traditional strict-liability theory of recovery for claims of manufacturing defect but, with respect to claims of design defect and inadequate warnings, incorporates an explicit balancing exercise that is more akin to a negligence analysis.[18]

Section 2 adopts a reasonableness-based, risk-utility balancing test as the standard for adjudging the defectiveness of product designs and warnings. It also makes clear that even a dangerous product is not defective unless there is proof of a reasonable alternative design (see ALI, 1998, §2, comment d). Comments to §2 also specify that the risk-benefit balancing done to judge product design must be done in light of knowledge attainable at the time the product was distributed. The comments also suggest that industry practice and the state of the art are relevant to the balancing analysis. With regard to warnings, §2

---

[18] §2 of ALI (1998) states,

> A product is defective when, at the time of sale or distribution, it contains a manufacturing defect, is defective in design, or is defective because of inadequate instructions or warnings. A product: (1) contains a manufacturing defect when the product departs from its intended design even though all possible care was exercised in the preparation and marketing of the product; (2) is defective in design when the foreseeable risks of harm posed by the product could have been reduced or avoided by the adoption of a reasonable alternative design by the seller or other distributor, or a predecessor in the commercial chain of distribution, and the omission of the alternative design renders the product not reasonably safe; (3) is defective because of inadequate instructions or warnings when the foreseeable risks of harm posed by the product could have been reduced or avoided by the provision of reasonable instructions or warnings by the seller or other distributor, or a predecessor in the commercial chain of distribution, and the omission of the instructions or warnings renders the product not reasonably safe.

states that a seller is not liable for failing to warn of known risks and risk-avoidance measures that should be obvious.

Strict product liability is probably the theory most often used by plaintiffs in suits against manufacturers involving the design of automobiles. As such, it will play a central role in litigation over the responsibility for crashes associated with AV technologies. In the wake of a crash involving an automobile with AV technologies, victims may argue that the car's technology was defective in some way. How these principles are applied will depend, however, on the type of product defect alleged.

Types of Defectiveness

Originally, product-liability case law and doctrine did not distinguish among kinds of defect. Over time, however, three categories of defect emerged: manufacturing defect, design defect, and failure to warn.

Manufacturing Defects. A product is said to have a manufacturing defect, according to §2(a) of ALI (1998), if it "departs from its intended design even though all possible care was exercised in the preparation and marketing of the product." Manufacturing defects can be divided into two types. First, the manufacturer can construct the product using flawed raw materials (e.g., unduly brittle steel used in a wheel). Second, the manufacturer can assemble the raw materials in an erroneous way—for example, by accidentally severing an important electrical cable during the manufacturing process. In either case, the product does not meet the manufacturer's own design specification.

If a plaintiff can prove a manufacturing defect by showing that a particular product does not meet the manufacturer's own specifications, the manufacturer has very few defenses and is usually found liable. But as quality process improvement techniques continue to spread within the automobile industry, the number of conventional manufacturing defects in automobiles is likely to continue to decrease (Dassbach, 1994).

Unless a particular AV technology relies on a particular part that is prone to defectiveness (e.g., a sensor with a high rate of defect), we do not anticipate significant litigation around manufacturing defects.

In cases where manufacturing defects do occur and lead to crashes, of course, plaintiffs will generally recover.

Design Defects. An allegation of a design defect submits that the design of the product itself is defective. In the automotive context, plaintiffs often allege that a vehicle was not sufficiently crashworthy—that it did not adequately protect its occupants during a crash. As vehicles get better at actually avoiding crashes rather than surviving them, the concept of crashworthiness may need to evolve.

Courts have used two principal tests for defectiveness of design: consumer expectations and cost-benefit. The consumer-expectation test was explained by one court as follows (*Donegal Mutual Insurance v White Consolidated Industries*, 2006):

> A product is defective in design or formulation when it is more dangerous than an ordinary consumer would expect when used in an intended or reasonably foreseeable manner. Moreover, the question of what an ordinary consumer expects in terms of the risks posed by the product is generally one for the trier of fact.

Comment i to §402A of ALI (1977) defines *unreasonably dangerous* as, in part, an issue of consumer expectations:

> i. Unreasonably Dangerous. The rule stated in this Section applies only where the defective condition of the product makes it unreasonably dangerous to the user or consumer. Many products cannot possibly be made entirely safe for all consumption, and any food or drug necessarily involves some risk of harm, if only from overconsumption. Ordinary sugar is a deadly poison to diabetics, and castor oil found use under Mussolini as an instrument of torture. That is not what is meant by "unreasonably dangerous" in this section. The article sold must be dangerous to an extent beyond that which would be contemplated by the ordinary consumer who purchases it, with the ordinary knowledge common to the community as to its characteristics.

While the consumer-expectation test is still used by some jurisdictions, many have abandoned it as unworkable.

The consumer-expectation test might result in substantial liability for the manufacturers of AV technologies simply because consumers may have unrealistic expectations about the capabilities of these technologies (e.g., *Hisrich v Volvo Cars of North America* [2000]: In a product-liability suit following air-bag deployment leading to a fatality, an instruction was warranted on the consumer-expectation test under Ohio law). A definition of *design defect* that relies primarily on consumer expectations may result in finding many design defects and lead to substantial manufacturer liability. Managing consumer expectations to prevent reliance that exceeds the capacities of these technologies will be important to minimize the number of crashes and reduce liability.

The cost-benefit (sometimes also called *risk-utility*) test is used by many courts to determine whether a design is defective. It attempts to weigh the benefits, or utility, provided by the particular design against the costs, or risks, associated with it. However, the precise factors that courts use in conducting a cost-benefit analysis to determine whether a design is defective vary by jurisdiction.

Current liability law on design defects may hinder the efficient adoption of AV technologies. Suppose, for example, that a particular type of "autobrake" crash-avoidance technology works to prevent crashes 80 percent of the time. The other 20 percent of the time, however, the technology does not work and the crash occurs as it would have in the absence of the technology. Victims in those crashes may sue the manufacturer and argue that the product was defective because it failed to operate properly in their crashes. Under existing liability doctrine, they have a plausible argument: The product did not work as designed (manufacturing defect). A manufacturer facing the decision whether to employ such a technology in its vehicles might very well decide not to, purely on the basis of expected liability costs.

Yet, the social benefits of this technology are likely to be substantial (see Parchomovsky and Stein, 2008, arguing that current tort law inefficiently deters innovation and suggesting reforms). An 80-percent decline (or even a 10-percent decline) in even a subcategory of crashes could save many lives and billions of dollars. The existing liability regime does a poor job of aligning private incentives with the public good in this kind of situation.

One approach to this problem is to integrate a cost-benefit analysis into the standard for liability as discussed earlier; this integration has the potential to reduce manufacturer liability because it allows the consideration of the benefits in reduced crash costs that are associated with this technology. If the cost-benefit analysis is permitted to include these benefits, tort liability for crashes that result from AV technologies is unlikely. This is because it seems probable that the adoption of these technologies is far more likely to reduce human error and traffic crashes than cause them. In the long run, this may be the socially optimal solution.

But while this may be appropriate calculation of the long-run socially optimal solution, it may also undermine incentives for safer product design in the short run. Suppose that an auto manufacturer has a choice between two AV technologies, one of which is much safer but only slightly more expensive. If the courts adopt a cost-benefit analysis that includes the benefits of the crashes eliminated by an AV technology, it may be that the manufacturer will not be found liable regardless of whether it chooses the safer or more dangerous technology. By focusing on the long-run costs and benefits to society of the adoption of AV technologies, the courts may undermine shorter-run opportunities for efficient safety. In this way, conducting the liability cost-benefit analysis by including more costs and benefits may undermine other incentives for safety in the shorter run.[19]

To maximize the social benefits of this technology, policymakers need to structure the liability and regulatory regime to encourage the development of this technology without undermining marginal incentives for safety. Careful thought and further research may be necessary to determine which costs and benefits should be included in the cost-benefit analysis that accompanies product liability.

Human-Computer Interaction

We also anticipate litigation around the optimal way to monitor and integrate the driver for those transitional technologies that are designed

---

[19] See Anderson (2007) for a fuller discussion of the way in which the tort system attempts to balances optimization in the short and long runs.

to function with a supervisory driver. This issue poses particular difficulties because alert supervision of the driving function without actively participating may be very difficult for humans, who are prone to lose attention when not directly engaged. Finding an appropriate way to allow these technologies to minimize human error without provoking dangerous overreliance on them may prove difficult and prompt post-crash litigation.[20] It will probably be in automakers' interest to continue to focus attention on the need for a responsible driver to monitor the AV technologies, even after the technologies mature sufficiently to allow truly autonomous operation. To the extent possible, automakers will want to preserve the social and legal norm that crashes are primarily the moral and legal responsibility of the driver, both to minimize their own liability and to ensure safety.[21]

Finally, it is also possible that auto manufacturers will be sued for *failing* to incorporate AV technologies in their vehicles. This theory has met with mixed success in the automotive field because manufacturers have sometimes successfully argued that state tort remedies were preempted by federal regulation. We discuss preemption and the relationship between regulation and tort below.

Warning Defects. Products can also be found defective for their failure to include appropriate warnings. If there is a hidden danger in the product, the manufacturer has an obligation to warn of the danger. If it fails to do so, the product can be found defective as a result of its failure to warn.

There is likely to be substantial litigation over the extent to which warnings are appropriate with AVs. Should a manufacturer warn a consumer that she should not use a laptop computer while using ACC and the lane keeping function? The plaintiff in such a case could argue that the cost of such a warning would be trivial and might save numerous lives. The defendant could argue that it is impossible to anticipate every

---

[20] Use of multiple driver-assistance systems at the same time also increases this risk. So, for example, relying on lane keeping function and ACC together may pose risks of overreliance that would not be raised if only one of these technologies was used at a time.

[21] Kyle Graham (2012) notes a tendency to "blame the user" for new technologies even when the technology seems clearly defective.

situation that could require a warning and that the instruction manual that accompanied the car clearly set out the limits of the automobile's AV systems.[22]

New vehicle communications technology may also change the duty to warn. Many stakeholders anticipate that cars will be wirelessly connected to the Internet to permit software and other updates to the car's operating systems. In theory, this will allow near instantaneous warnings to be sent by the manufacturers to any category or subcategory of cars relatively easily. This may increase the manufacturers' duty to warn consumers of any risks that they become aware of, because it will be more reasonable (and less expensive) for the manufacturers to do so (Smith, 2013a).

Simultaneously, the enormous amounts of data about the car's operation and its environment potentially available to the manufacturer may increase the ability of the manufacturer to identify systematic problems with particular subcategories of its products (Smith, 2013a). This may also increase the manufacturer's liability.

Effect of Regulation on Liability and Preemption

Relevant regulations, engineering standards, and industry custom are usually admissible but not dispositive as to whether a defendant met the appropriate standard of care (Owen, Montgomery, and Davis, 2007, p. 290).[23] So, in most state tort cases, the plaintiff or defendant can introduce the existence of a state or federal regulation, standard, or evidence of industry custom in arguing his or her case. The jury is free to consider this evidence in determining whether the defendant satisfied the appropriate standard of care. Contrary to this general rule, §4 of ALI (1998) indicates that, in product-liability cases, a manufacturer's *failure* to adhere to a relevant rule should give rise to liability

---

[22] Inquiry into the proper role of warnings also raises the issue of preemption, discussed in the next section.

[23] As explained in the next section, SAE standards governing AV technologies are beginning to emerge, but there are few federal regulations at this point.

in a design-defect or failure-to-warn case but that the manufacturer's adherence to the relevant rule does not preclude liability.[24]

In the case of federal preemption, however, compliance with federal regulations can completely absolve a defendant of liability in state courts in certain circumstances.[25] Preemption occurs when a court finds that Congress intended to preempt state laws that are inconsistent with the regulations enacted by the designated agency. This can occur when a federal statute either explicitly preempts inconsistent state law (*express preemption*) or implicitly does so by the creation of a regulation that is inconsistent with state tort law. So, for example, product manufacturers may argue that federal safety regulations preempt inconsistent state tort law and preclude lawsuits by injured plaintiffs.

Preemption is a controversial subject. Proponents of the doctrine argue that an expert federal agency is better suited to weighing the appropriate advantages and disadvantages of a product design or warning than a lay jury, and that it is unfair to subject product manufacturers to potentially 51 different and sometimes conflicting sets of requirements, depending on the particular holdings of juries in 51 jurisdictions.

Opponents of preemption argue that extinguishing state tort law rights is a violation of states' rights. They quote U.S. Supreme Court Justice Louis D. Brandeis, who famously sought to leave open the possibility that "a single courageous State may, if its citizens choose, serve as a laboratory; and try novel social and economic experiments without risk to the rest of the country" (*New State Ice Co. v Liebman*, 1932, Jus-

---

[24] §4,"Noncompliance and Compliance with Product Safety Statutes or Regulations," of ALI (1998) states,

> In connection with liability for defective design or inadequate instructions or warnings: (a) a product's noncompliance with an applicable product safety statute or administrative regulation renders the product defective with respect to the risks sought to be reduced by the statute or regulation; and (b) a product's compliance with an applicable product safety statute or administrative regulation is properly considered in determining whether the product is defective with respect to the risks sought to be reduced by the statute or regulation, but such compliance does not preclude as a matter of law a finding of product defect.

[25] This doctrine is based on the Supremacy Clause of the U.S. Constitution (Art. VI, cl. 2).

tice Brandeis dissenting). Opponents of federal preemption argue that not only does federal preemption stifle this "laboratory" and regulatory innovation, it also permits powerful industries to snuff out traditional rights of action and hobble the states' concurrent regulatory authority.

Another, more fundamental argument against preemption of state tort law remedies arises from the function of the tort law system itself. If state tort law exists only to serve as an efficient means to regulate risk, preemption may make sense if the federal government can do a better job at doing so. In recent years, Jules Coleman and several other tort theorists have argued that an important function of tort law is to provide corrective justice—to provide a procedure to right wrongs (Coleman, 1992; Zipursky, 2003). Federal preemption eliminates the state remedy without replacing it with any equivalent procedure. Accordingly, if one believes that an important function of tort law is corrective justice or civil recourse, one might be skeptical of federal preemption.

Implied preemption has arisen in the automotive context in litigation over a manufacturer's failure to install air bags. In *Geier v American Honda Motor Co.* (2000), the U.S. Supreme Court found that state tort litigation over a manufacturer's failure to install air bags was preempted by the National Traffic and Motor Vehicle Safety Act (U.S. Code, 1966). More specifically, the court found that FMVSS 208, promulgated by the U.S. DOT, required manufacturers to equip some but not all of their 1987 model-year vehicles with passive restraints. Because the plaintiffs' theory that the defendants were negligent under state tort law for failing to include air bags was inconsistent with the objectives of FMVSS 208, the court held that the state lawsuits were preempted. However, that case was narrowly decided, 5–4.

Since that decision, the court has rejected several implied preemption claims. For example, in *Wyeth v Levine* (2009), the court rejected, 6–3, the claim that the FDA's approval of a pharmaceutical drug's labeling preempted a state law claim on behalf of an injured patient. In the FMVSS context, the court considered a claim of preemption raised by an auto manufacturer that argued that the FMVSS concerning seat belt use preempted a state tort suit against the manufacturer for failure to install three-point seat belts in the middle position of a minivan's third row. In *Williamson v Mazda* (2011), the Supreme Court held 8–0 that implied preemption did not apply.

There has been very little regulation promulgated by NHTSA with respect to AV technologies. Should NHTSA enact such regulation, it is likely that manufacturers would argue that state tort law claims should be disallowed as preempted and inconsistent with the objectives of the regulation. However, the recent decisions of *Wyeth* and *Williamson* suggest that the Supreme Court will be cautious in finding state court tort claims preempted absent evidence of express legislative intent.

Explicit Legislative Preemption

Congress could pass legislation to prevent state court tort litigation in this area in several ways. First, lawmakers could flatly limit liability for AV technology. While it is uncommon, there are several precedents for such technology-specific legislation. In 1957, Congress passed the Price-Anderson Nuclear Industries Indemnity Act to reduce the liability of the nascent nuclear energy industry (U.S. Code, 1957). In 1986, the National Childhood Vaccine Injury Act was passed to limit liability for drug companies and create a no-fault compensation system for those injured by vaccines (U.S. Code, 1986). In 1990, Congress created the Oil Spill Liability Trust Fund, which limits liability for oil companies (U.S. Code, 1990). In 1994, the General Aviation Revitalization Act of 1994 created a statute of repose and immunized makers of small aircraft against liability for planes after 18 years from manufacture even if negligence was shown (U.S. Code, 1994). In 1999, Congress restricted liability for problems related to "Y2K" (Public Law 106-37).[26] In 2005, Congress passed the Public Readiness and Emergency Preparedness Act, which protected drug manufacturers from liability for vaccine-caused injuries during a declared public health emergency (U.S. Code, 2005). Internationally, the Warsaw convention of 1929 limited liability

---

[26] The Year 2000 Responsibility and Readiness Act (Public Law 106-37) limits Y2K liability by requiring clear and convincing evidence of damage and limiting damages to the lesser of $250,000 or three times compensatory damages; it also requires proportional rather than joint and several liability.

for personal injuries (and lost baggage) for international plane travel. This had the effect of capping airlines' liability for crashes on international routes. Congress could certainly pass a bill that simply limited liability for these technologies. However, there would surely be difficult line-drawing necessary to determine precisely when such liability exemptions should apply.

Second, Congress could provide a reinsurance backstop. A slightly different model for facilitating risk spreading was seen in the Terrorism Risk Insurance Act of 2002 (U.S. Code, 2002). Rather than a liability exemption, this legislation created a federal backstop reinsurance program to promote the availability of insurance for terrorist attacks, which became much harder to obtain after the September 11, 2001, terrorist attacks. Similarly, Congress might pass a similar bill to create a reinsurance backstop if the novelties of liability for AVs pose an unusual problem.

Conclusion

We have examined how the U.S. tort system applies to AV technologies and how that might affect the efficient adoption of these technologies. The existing liability regime does not seem to present unusual liability concerns for owners or drivers of vehicles equipped with AV technologies. In fact, the decrease in the number of crashes and the associated lower insurance costs that these technologies are expected to bring about will generally encourage the adoption of this technology by drivers and automobile insurance companies.

In contrast, manufacturer liability is expected to increase, and this may lead to inefficient delays in the adoption of these technologies. Manufacturers may be held responsible under several theories of liability for systems that aid the driver but leave him or her in total or partial control, under the claim that drivers were misinformed about the true capabilities of the system. Warnings and consumer education will play a crucial role in managing manufacturer liability for these systems. Manufacturers are likely to understate system capabilities during advertising, educate owners when purchasing vehicles with these capabilities, and require drivers to acknowledge that they understand the limitations in some way before the technologies can be activated. Some manufacturers have taken further steps to ensure that drivers understand and maintain their responsibility for driving by monitoring driver behavior when these technologies are activated and warning the driver or deactivating the technology if the driver appears to be inattentive. Manufacturers are likely to push for continued driver responsibility for the actions of the car.[27]

Manufacturers' liability concerns may slow the introduction of socially beneficial technologies. This delay may be perfectly appropriate for technologies that are extremely complex, such as vehicles that are fully autonomous, where there would be enormous difficulties proving complete reliability, given the range of conditions in which the vehicle will need to operate. On the other hand, this may be problematic for some technologies that provide benefits some of the time and do no additional harm otherwise. One approach to this problem is to integrate a more encompassing cost-benefit analysis into the standard for liability: It has the potential to reduce manufacturer liability because it allows consideration of the benefits in reduced crash costs associated with this technology. But it is difficult to specify the appropriate sets of costs and benefits that should be considered.[28]

Another possible approach is explicit or implicit regulatory preemption—requiring manufacturers to incorporate the most-promising forms of this technology by regulatory fiat but simultaneously exempting the manufacturers from state court liability.

Manufacturers themselves may be able to affect the liability by offering transportation as a service rather than a product. Bryant Walker Smith has suggested that manufacturers may offer automated

---

[27] The shift from a focus on the driver as being primarily responsible for crashes to the vehicle manufacturer will be complete if and when driverless cars are introduced. In such a case, there is obviously no conventional "driver" to hold responsible.

[28] Another possible solution is for a regulatory agency to require the use of certain safety technologies but to simultaneously exempt, through preemption, manufacturers from liability associated with that technology. This may be appropriate for safety technologies whose overall benefits are very clear, but the disadvantages of preemption are discussed in this chapter.

driving as an ongoing service product, rather than a good that is purchased and owned (Smith, 2013b). By doing so, manufacturers may be able to use contract law to limit their liability and better control the way their products are used. Scott (2008) discusses the way this issue has arisen in the software industry. It may also allow the manufacturer (or a car-sharing company) to serve as the auto insurer of its customers and capture the expected surplus as crash rates decline.

Uncertainty itself over the magnitude of the liability risks may also deter and delay introduction of these technologies. This can create a catch-22 because the court system can resolve this uncertainty only when claims are actually brought and litigated, which, of course, requires that the technology be introduced. Nonetheless, we anticipate that as this technology is gradually introduced into the marketplace, the legal standards will be clarified.

CHAPTER EIGHT

Guidance for Policymakers and Conclusion

As discussed in Chapter Two, AV technology offers considerable promise to improving social welfare along a number of dimensions. From safety to congestion to the built environment, AV technology offers potential to improve social welfare. While there are also some important disadvantages and risks associated with this technology, these seem limited compared with the potential gains.

But the path to AVs realizing this improved social welfare is not preordained. The history of technology in general—and transportation in particular—is littered with promising ideas that never achieved widespread adoption.[1] And even if widespread adoption eventually occurs, thousands may be injured or killed in crashes if that adoption is unnecessarily delayed. Conversely, a hastily enacted mandate for suboptimal technology could lead to enormous lost social welfare.

This technology is likely to generate many positive externalities—benefits to those other than the purchasers. Since they do not accrue to the purchasers, these positive externalities will not be incorporated in economic demand for this technology. The result may be a market failure and the potential for a less than socially optimal outcome. In this chapter, we discuss those risks and offer some tentative suggestions for policymakers.

---

[1] For example, in 1966, it seemed a truism that supersonic transport planes would shuttle businessmen around the country. A RAND researcher predicting trends in air transportation focused not on whether supersonic transport would be adopted, but whether they might be powered by nuclear or hydrogen engines. Raymond (1966).

Risks from Market Failure

One important uncertainty is the precise business model for selling this technology to consumers. Many of the existing demonstrations of AV technology involve suites of sensors that currently cost tens of thousands of dollars and would double or triple the cost of most cars. It seems unlikely that consumer demand would be substantial at such a cost. While most stakeholders we interviewed were confident that substantial price reductions will occur, no one seemed particularly confident of a particular technological roadmap. For example, Elon Musk of Tesla recently suggested that a camera-based system, less expensive than Google's lidar-based system, might be the way to go forward (Ohnsman, 2013). But it is unclear whether such a system would be sufficiently reliable or safe. While the combination of the existing technologies of ACC and lane keeping could create Level 2 automation relatively simply, it is unclear how much consumers would be willing to pay for a systems that requires constant vigilance of the road and the ability to take over the driving task in a split second.[2]

Despite the current enthusiasm for AV technology and the amount of research among automakers and others, it is possible that it will not become widely adopted, simply because it will be too expensive. Absent sufficient demand, economies of scale and network effects will not reduce the marginal cost and the technology might wither. The lack of a viable business model has doomed some earlier efforts at road vehicle automation.

In and of itself, this would not be remarkable or cause for concern. The history of technology is filled with dead-ends and promising leads that ended up never being economical to bring to production. In a free market economy, the fact that consumers are not willing to pay for a product suggests that the product does not create sufficient consumer surplus. But in this case, because of the positive externalities the technology could create, it is possible net social welfare could be impaired.

---

[2]   It is possible such a system might be more valued by consumers facing traffic jams regularly, but it is still unclear whether consumer demand is sufficient to justify introduction.

In Chapter Two, we surveyed some of the general benefits of this technology: reducing crashes and the costs of congestion, and improving efficiency. Some of these benefits are likely to directly benefit the potential purchaser of this technology. However, many of the benefits will spill over to others. For example, if AVs result in congestion reduction, the benefits will help anyone on the road, whether or not they have purchased vehicles with this technology. Similarly, reducing crashes will aid not only those in vehicles with this technology but also the would-be victims in vehicles without this technology. This spillover benefit, or positive externality, explains why relying purely upon the free market may not maximize social welfare.[3]

Some of the expected benefits of this technology are in the form of positive externalities, but not all are. For example, the expected reduction in congestion is a benefit to other motorists, but the reduction in the cost of congestion—because the driver can do other things—is a benefit to the vehicle operator. If there is an increase in congestion because of additional vehicle miles traveled, a negative externality would occur. More research on precisely estimating the positive and negative externalities would be a first step toward determining whether a subsidy is economically justified.

Such a market failure might justify some form of government subsidy to encourage adoption and use. The federal government has provided a substantial tax credit to purchasers of electric cars, which is, in part, justified by a similar market failure. A similar subsidy might be justified in this context. The precise form of this subsidy (deduction, tax credit, etc.) and whether it should be provided to consumers or manufacturers should be subject to further study and research. Similarly, the optimal amount of subsidy (if any) is an interesting question that should be subject to further research.

As noted in Chapter Two, AV technology is likely to have some negative effects. By reducing costs of congestion (because drivers may do other things), AV technology may lead to increased vehicle

---

[3] Many of these positive externalities are really just reductions of the negative externalities that conventional driving imposes upon others. For example, as noted in Chapter Two, driving a car imposes substantial congestion costs upon other motorists.

miles traveled, congestion, and emissions. These are also externalities (because the driver does not bear the cost), but negative ones. To align market forces with appropriate policy outcomes, policymakers might consider using a VMT-based taxation system.

Risks from Regulation

We are likely to see a variety of AV concepts with different operating constraints enter the market. Some of these concepts may require human drivers and the vehicle to share the driving task. Policymakers must consider how to regulate both the vehicles and the operators of those vehicles to ensure safety and promote benefits of these technologies, without hindering their development. While the FCC decision over the spectrum used by DSRC has received considerable attention, there are also other important policy issues raised by telematics and communications.

Vehicle performance is traditionally tested at the federal level by NHTSA, and driver performance is traditionally tested at the state level by DMVs. AVs—in which the driver *is* the vehicle—complicate these traditional roles.

As discussed in Chapter Four, developing performance tests for each vehicle concept of operation may be prohibitively costly, particularly at the state level. Simultaneously, some stakeholders with whom we spoke expressed concerns that premature regulation on the state level may result in a crazy-quilt of different, and perhaps incompatible, requirements. Attempting to meet state regulations could increase costs and make the technology uneconomical.

NHTSA recently expressed some caution about regulations on the state level, noting that "[p]articularly in light of the rapid evolution and wide variations in self-driving technologies, we do not believe that detailed regulation of these technologies is feasible at this time at the federal or state level" (NHTSA, 2013).

Yet, there are also concerns about performance testing at the federal level. NHTSA could set performance standards that require a particular series of technological approaches to AVs. Regulating vehicles at the federal level to ensure conformance to the vast array of different and changing state transportation laws may be extremely difficult.

Some have expressed concerns that regulation of this kind would simultaneously stifle technology. Early standards might prematurely discourage the development of alternative approaches. One technology company we contacted had expressed concern about this risk, given the uncertainties and speed of development in the field. However, NHTSA's recently issued policy statement recognizes that "regulation of the technical performance of automated vehicles is premature at this time," and that "premature regulation can run the risk of putting the brakes on the evolution toward increasingly better vehicle safety technologies" (NHTSA, 2013). This suggests that this risk is minimal, at least for now.

Given the lack of demonstrated problems with autonomous or self-driving vehicle use, we think state lawmakers would be wise to refrain from passing laws or developing regulations in this area. As NHTSA noted, evolution is occurring too rapidly and there are too many uncertainties for productive regulation at this time. Instead, we strongly encourage policymakers to collaborate closely with insurers, manufacturers, consumer groups, and others to develop standards and regulations over time, as the technology matures.

It would also be useful for state lawmakers to consider updating distracted driving laws to accommodate AV technologies, as discussed in Chapter Four. The creation of a communications platform in AVs that can be used for driver assistance and safety reasons may also be used for voice communications, navigation assistance, and infotainment. More than one stakeholder we interviewed has suggested there may be conflicts with state distracted driving laws and regulations, particularly concerning navigation systems. Distracted driving laws vary widely from state to state, and could pose a challenge for development of a standard AV communications platform.

Similarly, stakeholders have explained that the design of AV communications platforms will need to be standardized, at least through "best practices," so developers can address a single platform design instead of many. According to several stakeholders, the size and type of processor is a developmental cost issue that could either promote or impede deployment of AVs to the mass market. One stakeholder noted that OEMs are looking to U.S. DOT to help with such standardization, but that "mandate is considered a dirty word."

Many stakeholders we interviewed identified policy questions for state and federal regulators concerning data use and legal issues, such as how long AV data should be maintained and by whom. Corollary issues include whether and how AV data can be disposed of or destroyed, and the legal rights of the vehicle owner to have access to vehicle data. Stakeholders also raised the issue of whether data gathered, produced, or transmitted by AVs will be discoverable in legal proceedings. Data ownership and privacy issues related to AV communications are unsettled and present an important policy gap.

Finally, as described more fully in Chapter Four, the FCC faces a policy choice in its current Notice of Proposed Rulemaking between supporting enhanced Internet access and preventing potentially harmful interference to DSRC spectrum if it is shared by unlicensed devices. The 5.9 GHz spectrum band used by DSRC was designated by the FCC for use by "connected cars." This dilemma will persist until the effects of spectrum sharing in the 5.9 GHz band have been clearly demonstrated. The FCC will need to determine which course better serves the public interest, as expressed in the 1934 Communications Act.

Risks from Liability

Currently, the primary responsibility for crashes lies with vehicle drivers.[4] An extensive and comprehensive system of first- and third-party liability insurance centered on the driver is mandated in every state except New Hampshire. Americans spent roughly $157 billion on insurance for automobiles in 2009.

To some extent, the attribution of the "cause" of most crashes to drivers is arbitrary. After all, any crash has numerous antecedent conditions that are necessary for the crash to occur, and it is not dif-

---

[4] See Anderson, Heaton, and Carroll (2010) for a more thorough description of no-fault, tort liability, and the auto insurance system in the United States.

ficult to imagine a wide variety of parties affecting crash outcomes. For example, if automobiles were limited in speed to 30 mph, the rate of fatal crashes would almost surely decline. Yet we do not ordinarily attribute fatal crashes to the failure of car manufacturers to limit their products to 30 mph. As one of us has explored in more detail elsewhere (Anderson, 2007), the way in which tort law considers factors that "cause" a crash can be arbitrary.

As vehicles take on more of the driving functions that were historically the responsibility of the driver, there may be a shift in our thinking about accident responsibility. Rather than immediately attribute accidents to drivers, we may be more inclined to blame manufacturers or perhaps Tier 1 suppliers.

Manufacturers may fear this shift in crash liability, since it may mean millions or billions of dollars in new liability. As a result, they may be reluctant to introduce new technology that might advance this new paradigm despite the fact it could save thousands of lives. Alternatively, manufacturers might price the new technology to incorporate their expected liability risks, which might greatly reduce the demand for the technology and either slow or halt adoption.

This is particularly true of Level 3 and Level 4 technologies designed to permit the driver to attend to other tasks. As discussed elsewhere, these will pose particular difficulties with respect to human-computer interaction and the transition back to human-controlled driving.

While several manufacturers (Ford, Volvo, and Mercedes-Benz) have introduced a variety of automated safety features in some of their vehicles, these have been exclusively premium vehicles and it is unclear whether these will trickle down to less expensive models.[5] And these technologies have not offered true autonomy, so the more difficult liability issues are not raised.

Even assuming that automakers do end up with more liability for crashes, it may be that this cost can easily be passed on to consumers,

---

[5] Historically, it has taken approximately 30 years from the time a new safety feature is introduced by a manufacturer until the time that that safety feature is in 95 percent of registered automobiles (Highway Loss Data Institute, 2012).

who will presumably have to pay less for automobile insurance. If crash costs remain the same, a shift of liability from drivers to automakers may just mean a different form of insurance. Rather than purchasing insurance from car insurance firms, consumers will effectively be purchasing insurance for crashes from automakers, built into the price of the car. And, as explained in Chapter Two, it seems likely that crash incidence will decline substantially.

Another stakeholder we interviewed noted that these risks were insurable by automakers. So even if the shift to AV technology were to lead to increased automaker liability, automakers and their liability insurers would be in an excellent position to purchase insurance of their own for this particular risk.

In short, it is not clear that liability concerns justify any intervention at this point. However, if and when manufacturer liability proves an issue, policymakers could address this issue in several ways, as covered in the next five sections.

Federal Statute Limiting Tort

Congress could pass a statute that limited liability of car manufacturers (or immunized them completely) for certain categories of AV technology. Such an approach has some precedents, discussed in Chapter Seven. International air travel, nuclear power, and vaccines are all areas in which a promising technology received the subsidy of liability protection.

However, such an approach has a number of drawbacks. It is not clear that it would be politically feasible or that a bipartisan consensus exists to overrule the ordinary operation of tort law in such a potentially large sector of the U.S. economy. Difficult definitional issues are also likely to be raised: What, precisely, should count as an AV technology for the purposes of this statute? Finally, it is not at all clear that it would be good policy. Tort law compensates victims, creates incentives for safety, and provides victims with a societally sanctioned procedure to prove that they were wronged. It is not clear that altering this important institution is justified. Even if AV technology creates considerable positive externalities, it is not clear that altering the tort system is the best way to subsidize it.

Express Federal Regulatory Preemption

A more limited approach would be for Congress to ask NHTSA (or another agency) to issue detailed regulations concerning the manufacture of AVs and the appropriate performance standards that the technology must meet. Congress could indicate that such regulations would preempt the operation of state tort law.

While this approach is a bit more restrained than the first, it shares many of its faults; most notably, it is not clear that suspending the ordinary operation of tort law is justified.

Moreover, the technology is still evolving so quickly, it would be very difficult for NHTSA to issue appropriate performance standards. Several stakeholders who were knowledgeable about the regulatory process emphasized how difficult it would be to enact meaningful performance standards when the technology is evolving so quickly. A government transportation official we interviewed said the same thing. He examined the possible roles for the government to play, including education and other ways to narrow the focus of disputes. However, when it came to issuing standards, he thought it was extremely difficult to stay relevant, given the swift pace of technological change. Comparing government standards to "the elephant sitting on the mouse running a race," he said standards soon become obsolete and retard progress.

It may be that over time, that problem resolves itself—as the technology becomes more mature, appropriate performance standards may become clear to NHTSA. But we have not reached that point.

No-Fault Approach

The nation now has a substantial history with an alternative to conventional tort with respect to automobile crashes: no-fault. Currently the law in 12 states, the no-fault system allows crash victims to recover damages from their own auto insurers after a crash instead of having to seek recovery from another driver. In theory, this was supposed to reduce costs, and it was thought it would be easier to recover from one's own insurer than against another party. In practice, it has proved somewhat disappointing, with costs remaining higher than hoped (Anderson, Heaton, and Carroll, 2010).

However, if AV technology reduces the responsibility of the individual driver as expected, a no-fault approach may become more attractive. It might retain the model of having the individual car owner be fiscally responsible for crashes and preserving the vast existing "crash economy," of insurers and other parties, without having to make difficult determinations about responsibility between drivers, automobile makers, etc. This may make it less likely that manufacturers would face the increased liability costs that may slow the introduction of the technology. On the other hand, this also may be politically unrealistic.

Irrebuttable Presumption of Driver Control of Vehicle

Alternatively, a legislature, at either state or federal level, could pass a bill requiring that a single person be responsible for the control of the vehicle. This person could delegate that responsibility to the car, but would still be presumed to be in control of the vehicle in the case of a crash. We could retain the "driver as ultimately responsible party" paradigm no matter what the level of automation is. In this vision, every vehicle would have a "driver" who would be responsible, whether or not he or she was actually directly controlling the vehicle operation at any given moment. As noted above, the current attribution of crashes to drivers is somewhat arbitrary even now. This solution would simply preserve that attribution. As one AV developer we interviewed explained, "having an operator in control allows the industry to move forward."

One manufacturer we interviewed seemed to take this approach and emphasized that a driver would always be in ultimate control of the vehicle. This manufacturer, while quite willing to discuss various driver assistance mechanisms and an "autopilot" function, wanted to retain the "human driver as ultimate controller" paradigm of automotive control and was critical of Google for demonstrating a blind person using an AV. Similarly, Elon Musk of Tesla has suggested that the conceptual model should be an autopilot engaged by the driver rather than self-driving cars (Ohnsman, 2013).

This approach would preserve the existing infrastructure of compensation for crashes while making it less likely that automobile manufacturers would face substantially increased liability costs. However, it would still require legislative intervention.

Incorporation of Appropriate Cost-Benefit Tests in Liability Determinations

As discussed in Chapter Six, courts are increasingly likely to incorporate some form of cost-benefit analysis in making determinations about product-liability cases. In this context, as discussed in Chapter Two, a strong argument can be made that the benefits of AV technology and vehicle designs that employ them are substantial. Courts should continue to incorporate cost-benefit analyses into product-liability determinations and compare the expected costs of a conventional, driver-controlled vehicle with those of an AV when determining liability. We believe this will reflect the underlying principle that the technology should be permitted when it is superior to the average human driver.

While it is certainly possible that liability concerns may delay introduction of some of this technology, legislative intervention in the tort system is complex and difficult. While there are some policy interventions that might reduce this risk, it is not clear they outweigh their disadvantages. The tort system serves important social goals of providing incentives for safety and compensating the injured, and interventions to reduce liability may do more harm than good. In contrast, it is easier for courts to continue to incorporate cost-benefit analysis in product-liability determinations.

What Principles Should Guide Policymakers?

We think that the guiding principle for policymakers should be that AV technology should be permitted and encouraged if and when it is superior to average human drivers. So, for example, safety regulations and liability rules should be designed with this overarching guiding principle in mind. Similarly, this principle can provide some guidance to judges struggling with determining whether a particular design decision was reasonable in the context of a product-liability lawsuit.

This stands in contrast to an alternative approach of viewing AVs with more suspicion and requiring near perfection before introduction. Tort law has a long tradition of viewing new activities with some suspicion and requiring their adherents to bear all of the associated costs under the doctrine of ultrahazardous activity.[6] Similarly, the "reasonable person" test at the heart of much tort liability implies a preference for the status quo (Parchomovsky and Stein, 2008; Anderson, 2007).

This principle will, of course, require considerable judgment in application. There may be cases in which AV technology is superior to driver-operated vehicles in one dimension but not in another. In cases where the costs and benefits can be quantified, a rough attempt to measure the more important dimension can be made, but that might not always be possible (Sunstein, 1994). Despite its imperfections, we think that focusing on comparing AV technology to vehicles operated by human drivers will provide useful, principled guidance to policymakers as they confront a range of issues.

Policy Research Needs

We have highlighted many of the legal, technological, and social benefit issues involving a transition to AVs. Federal and state governments will come under increasing pressure to ensure the safety of vehicle automation and its integration with infrastructure, and to create an environment where new opportunities from these vehicles can be developed. It is clear that a large responsibility for addressing vehicle automation will reside with NHTSA, while fuel economy and emissions issues will require capabilities at the EPA. AV technology will be disruptive and crosscutting, and several research tasks arise:

- Develop more precise estimates of the costs and benefits of these technologies and determine whether they accrue to the operator of the vehicle or the public more broadly.
- Develop better estimates of the distributional consequences of AV technology. (What groups are likely to gain and what groups are likely to lose?)

---

[6] More precisely, "common usage" was an exception to liability for ultrahazardous activity. James (1949) discusses how novel activities were more likely to be considered ultrahazardous.

- What are lessons learned from the introduction of other vehicle technologies that can prepare NHTSA and EPA for this transition?
- What capabilities, enabled by both human capital and statutory authority, do NHTSA and EPA require to effectively serve the public interest and facilitate technology development in a rapidly evolving field?
- How will future fuel economy standards account for AV technology? And how will private and social costs and benefits be estimated?
- Further develop model legislation concerning AVs to avoid the "50-state patchwork" of laws that has been described by OEMs and other stakeholders as a serious concern for development and deployment of AVs.
- Analyze the advantages and disadvantages of explicit or implicit regulatory preemption (requiring manufacturers to incorporate the most-promising forms of AV technology by regulatory mandate but simultaneously exempting the manufacturers from state court liability).
- Analyze existing state "distracted driving" laws and whether they will need to be amended to accommodate AVs.
- Investigate the potential impact of AVs on travel modes, and how these changes may affect planners at all levels, especially state and federal DOTs.
- Identify, define, and examine existing models for transportation data management, as well as potential data needs for automated road vehicles. For each model identified, explore whether the model provides insight regarding how automated road vehicle data might be handled. Issues to be explored could include what parties may access personal location information, personally identifiable information, vehicle operation, etc., and how they can and cannot use these data. The latter question should include data access, sharing, and security. The research should then address how these issues would be resolved in the context of different stakeholders (e.g., vehicle manufacturers, data aggregators, government regulators, law enforcement, insurance, vehicle

owners and users). The research should highlight best practices and recommend how those might apply to regulations for automated road vehicles.

Conclusion

In this report, our goal was to provide a resource for policymakers interested in AV technology and the policy challenges it raises. First, we surveyed the technology's potential advantages and disadvantages. Overall, we concluded that the technology offers the potential of substantial gains in social welfare in crash reduction, congestion, cost of congestion, and pollution. Many of these benefits, however, accrue to the public at large rather than the purchaser of the technology. These positive externalities may justify policy interventions to align the private and public costs and benefits. In Chapter Three, we surveyed current state laws and legislative activity prompted by these developments. While these laws may prompt an important conversation between regulators and stakeholders, it is not clear that they are necessary at this point. After surveying the history of the development of the technology, we reviewed the current state of the technology and how it functions in Chapter Four. In Chapter Five, we examined the important role of telematics, the transfer of data to and from vehicles, and the technical and policy issues related to communications, particularly the issue posed by the FCC's consideration of sharing spectrum allocated to DSRC. In Chapter Six, we discussed government regulations and third-party standards and their effect on the development of this technology. In Chapter Seven, we reviewed the liability implications of AVs. While we think that AV technology will cause little problem with individual drivers and indeed will likely reduce insurance costs, the shift to AV technology may cause increased liability for automobile manufacturers, which may impede the adoption of this technology at considerable social cost. Finally, in this chapter, we summarized our suggestions for policymaking in this area.

Legal theorist Oona Hathaway has argued that law is path-dependent—the existing legal regime depends critically on decisions made earlier and that we might become "locked in" to an unnecessarily inefficient system (Hathaway, 2001). She offers the QWERTY keyboard as an example of an arguably subpar technology that became locked in as a result of the path-dependence of technological and economic development. In the field of AV technology, law and policy will play a critical role in shaping the paths of technological development and deployment. An early case, regulation, or other policy (or lack thereof) could permanently shape the development of this technology. These pathways may influence the course of development in this field for a long time. It is therefore important that policymakers get it as right as possible.

Unfortunately, this is quite hard. While AV technology appears a way of improving social welfare, we are still at a very early stage of development. As Yogi Berra famously noted, "It is tough to make predictions, especially about the future." This, we think, is ample grounds for humility. At this stage, there are many more questions than answers. While we have attempted to provide a useful overview of this area for policymakers and researchers, much work remains to be done.

At some point, policymaker intervention to align the private and public costs of this technology may be justified. But at this point aggressive regulatory action is premature and can probably do more harm than good.

Conclusions from Qualitative Interviews with Stakeholders

A. Methodology

We interviewed 30 stakeholders who represented different perspectives on AV development and deployment. These stakeholders included OEMs, the insurance industry, AV developers, global mobile communications companies, automotive market researchers, telematics developers and suppliers, state DMV officials, global automobile industry associations, global high-technology companies, lawyers for automobile manufacturers, technology industry associations, "infotainment" industry experts, Tier 1 automotive suppliers, international consulting firms, and transportation industry government officials. We used a structured interview approach, with a list of questions that were used to guide the discussions. The interviews were conducted by telephone and in face-to-face meetings between January 28, 2013, and October 2, 2013. Each interview lasted approximately one hour. Most interviews involved one respondent; approximately one-fifth involved more than one respondent.

B. Analysis

The principal goal of the interviews was to elicit insights about six factors that could either accelerate or inhibit deployment of AVs. These six factors are discussed at length in the report. Among other questions, we asked each interview subject:

- What policy risks or gaps do you see concerning U.S. liability law in relation to AVs?
- What policy risks or gaps do you anticipate concerning licensing of AVs?
- What policy risks or gaps do you anticipate concerning insurance law in respect to AVs?
- What concerns do you have about privacy protection for data obtained and used by AVs?
- What are the communications issues you perceive, particularly concerning use of spectrum in the 5.9 GHz band, and DSRC operations?
- What are other risks or policy gaps that you think are critical for the deployment of AVs?

C. Key Factors

1. U.S. Liability Laws

An automobile industry association executive we interviewed about AVs stated succinctly, "OEMs will not shut up about liability."

One OEM executive whom we spoke with stated that in terms of liability, "the driver always has to be there and be responsible." Even in the OEM's test AV vehicles, there is always a driver in the driver's seat. This OEM executive thought that the transition to AVs would be an evolutionary process of driver assist systems. The key question OEMs have concerning AVs is, "who's responsible for what," according to an OEM executive we interviewed. One OEM executive suggested that the best solution to liability issues was federal preemption, and gave the example of medical vaccines.

An AV developer we spoke with said limiting liability for self-driving vehicles is probably not realistic. The developer commented that OEMs see liability as risk; therefore, their technologies all include a driver. The developer stated, "we will never make a car that doesn't have a driver." The developer explained that by keeping the driver in the loop, it maintains that current liability model.

A global high-technology company executive thought that an ISO standard concerning "Functional Risks," ISO 26262 for automobiles, was important to reduce liability. He said if auto manufacturers adhere to ISO standards, they can argue they are operating at the state of the art or industry, and have observed mechanisms for functional safety. The executive we interviewed thought this was a key area for development, stating that standards (such as new ISO specifications) and best practices go hand in hand to reduce liability.

Similarly, this executive pointed out that in aerospace applications, such as commercial airliners, there are three systems for critical functions, each separately engineered and which provide triple redundancy. He noted that it will be important to find the right level of redundancy in AVs as a way to control liability.

Two global technology company executives and an automobile association executive raised the issue that there needs to be some form of liability protection for the AV industry, and cited precedents from the nuclear reactor industry, medical vaccine development, the aerospace industry, and the Warsaw convention (which concerns airlines and plane crashes).

A mobile communications provider stated that liability concerns extend to everyone, from software makers to infrastructure operators—since it is early in the AV industry's development, it is a looming issue for all stakeholders. The liability issues appear to be increasing from the communications side as more onboard services are made available (e.g., through OnStar in GM cars), and "distracted driving" is being linked to "infotainment."

A navigation system executive we interviewed said his company withholds a certain percentage of its profits to prepare for liability or warranty litigation; so far, there have been no cases filed against the company. He noted that the company has legal agreements with its suppliers and customers to limit liability and warranty claims.

A technology industry advocacy group we interviewed pointed out state-to-state differences concerning AVs and automobile liability issues. Some states, she noted, have contributory negligence standards.

Lawyers for OEMs stated that the key issue for AV liability was "where does the fault lie." They hypothesized that AV technology might reduce common forms of accidents, but might result in many more fatalities if something goes wrong with the AV technology. These lawyers stated that liability issues could definitely impede AV development and deployment. A Tier 1 executive said he was dubious about the approach to liability taken by NHTSA, and that AV technologies were comparable to "today's active safety warning systems."

A global technology executive summarized the issue: "How do we create a policy environment and a liability environment that allows autonomous vehicle technology to emerge"?

2. Licensing of AVs

One of the OEM executives we interviewed observed that it does not make a lot of sense for there to be different AV laws and licensing regimes in California, Nevada, Florida, and Michigan. The executive also said the patchwork of state laws is potentially problematic. Specifically, it would be an inhibitor to deployment to have to recertify an AV in each state.

An AV developer we interviewed said licensing is "not a huge issue" and that "having an operator in control allows the industry to move forward." He observed that states want to redefine AVs in a particular way, and said technology issues are in vogue in state legislatures, so they seem to be passing bills without considering the technology.

3. Insurance

An AV developer said that while he did not see insurance as being an inhibitor to the deployment of AVs, it was probably not an accelerator, and the transmission of liability from drivers to OEMs is an "insurable risk."

A global technology company executive said there may be compelling value propositions offered by insurance companies or OEMs to share information. He said, "If you provide enough value, people will give all kinds of stuff away." One of his colleagues noted that insurance should be analyzed from a short-, medium- and long-term perspective as far as being an accelerator or inhibitor. In the short term, insurance costs go up—it may cost $5,000 to fix a fender with a sensor. In the medium term, costs go down as accidents decrease. For the longer term, the AV industry needs to prove the technology reduces crashes. She added that in the future, the types of accidents might change, as well as their frequency and severity—it is too soon to tell.

The insurance executive we spoke with commented that there may be fewer accidents but owners might need more insurance for comprehensive coverage and theft. He concurred that the cost to repair AVs would affect the cost of insurance in the short run. But he also said this was not an insurmountable problem, and could be ameliorated by the design and installation of AV equipment. He said testing of AVs was going to be an important factor in insurance. It would need to be rigorous, and should be carried out by a public/private partnership, not the government.

A global technology executive commented that DSRC/crash prevention is the next step to reduce the cost of accidents. He speculated that the next layer of use of the technology will be a fast and correct response to an accident, using a "black box" that sends data and the driver's vital statistics to first responders. He also noted that with V2V technology, you could re-create and identify the causes of vehicle crashes. He thought DSRC technology will also be able to reduce fraud and stolen vehicles. The executive said that although DSRC will probably reduce the cost of insurance by around $380 per vehicle per year, he thought parents probably would invest in AVs that used DSRC to protect their teenage drivers.

The navigation system executive we interviewed said insurance companies such as Allstate and Progressive currently supply a "black box" for cars that tracks usage and provides an insurance discount based on driving performance. He said the equipment for the "black box" costs almost as much as the discount, so the value proposition was not very appealing. The market research executive we spoke with observed that there may be demographic issues with usage-based insurance. Some young people may be willing to surrender their privacy for reduced insurance rates, but older people may not.

4. Privacy Protection for Data

An OEM executive stated that privacy and security are key issues for AV development. She explained that a consortium of automakers is working through privacy and security issues related to V2V and V2I. For example, how does a vehicle verify outside information? There needs to be some kind of certification process. That raises the question of who will be the issuer of the certificate. It may be the government or a third party. Some people in government have asked the OEM whether there should be a tag on these data like a vehicle identification number (VIN). The OEM executive explained that all data coming out of their AVs are anonymized, if possible. Data being transmitted out of the car never includes personally identifiable information as it is transmitted. The OEM executive confirmed that EDR data are the property of the vehicle owner, unless the owner provides permission for someone to use the data or there is a court order. Another OEM executive observed that U.S. DOT thinks it has all the authority it needs, but it has a "blinkered view" that "privacy is someone else's problem." The OEM executives we interviewed said privacy concerns could be overcome but security issues were more difficult.

In contrast to the OEM executive's comments about data privacy, the insurance company executive we spoke with said the insurance company owns the data from its product that measures miles driven, times driven, and high-risk behavior. This is accomplished by special provisions in the customer's insurance contract.

A Tier 1 supplier suggested that personally identifiable information is "any data connected to a VIN."

The technology industry association executive we interviewed stated that advertising agencies, insurance companies, and trial lawyers all want data that reside in the EDR "black box." She predicts that AVs will produce "big data" and all of these same interests will want to obtain data from AVs and exploit it. Similarly, the automotive industry executive we interviewed said that if you want an eventual DSRC mandate, "you need heavy-duty privacy protection."

The AV developer that we interviewed stated that data collection is really important to make vehicles better, and insisted that there were effective ways to prevent personally identifiable data from being transmitted and to anonymize data. He explained that the data obtained from AVs stay within the developer's environment and are used to improve and update the AV model.

A global technology executive said that "many people want to get their hands on data." He explained that there was a pragmatic way to handle this issue: If someone owns the vehicle, that person owns the data that come with it. However, he acknowledged that some people may be willing to trade data for benefits. If an OEM wants data, it can provide benefits to a car owner to provide those data. We spoke about the data that are available from mobile apps on smartphones, and he said that GM and GENIVI are currently offering development kits for mobile apps that will be used within automobiles, so this will be a new source of data. He thinks that his company will be able to use software to permit customers to decide what data they wish to share and what data they wish to keep private.

The automobile association executive we interviewed said data security issues are still unaddressed for AVS. He expressed the need for a credentialing system, and outlined the challenges. One example is how to match all the certificates between and among automobiles in a V2V environment. Another problem he cited was that any protocol developed could probably be broken over a 10–20 year period. The executive stated that OEMs are looking for help from U.S. DOT on this issue, and it would be helpful if DOT would provide guidance. He said this is what was done with EDRs, and the guidance was followed by an eventual requirement. He added that "the equipment is cheap, it is the security overlay that's expensive," and stated that the situation is similar to an EDR, in that the size of the processor is the issue. An OEM will have to decide what sort of hardware to invest in, and the potential life cycle for such equipment. We further discussed the possibility of using AV data for individual tracking purposes, and he explained that to prevent tracking, the AV data are not associated with a VIN, and the certificate authority would be the only entity that has access to the data. This raised the question of who will control the entity that will be managing the security system for vehicle certification. He stated that it is unclear whether a central or distributed approach would be the best solution and needs further research.

An OEM executive raised concerns about employing the technologies used in autonomous and connected vehicles for law enforcement surveillance purposes, and questioned whether this needs to be addressed by NHTSA or the states.

A mobile communications provider said AV security needs to be in the "cloud." He noted that only a cloud-based solution could manage all of the media and data involved in an AV, and said whether a security system should be centralized or distributed was always a subject of debate. However, he stated that the need for security of on-vehicle data and vehicle systems and connections is extremely critical, and requires a good defense strategy. When asked about "who owns the data," he compared a car engine to the power meter on the side of a house, and said that some data, such as personal location, should be kept private, but other data about the car itself should be made available. He thought it will be possible to have aggregated "buckets of information," with the option to share personal data. An OEM executive noted, however, that "a car is not a laptop."

Another mobile communications provider we interviewed said security issues are not well understood and data ownership "still needs to be figured out." His concern was that, as AVs become more computerized and more connected, they provide another aspect of critical infrastructure and a potential target for a cyberattack. He said all of an AV's systems had to be designed to resist possible intrusion by hackers, and cited an example where hackers were able to access a car's electronic systems through a seemingly innocuous tire pressure gauge. He said security needs to apply to all communications paths into the car, whether it is Wi-Fi, LTE, or DSRC.

One pathway for data into and out of AVs will be through mobile apps. The technology industry association executive we spoke with said developers of mobile apps for AVs "are going to find themselves in FTC land," referring to the active role the Federal Trade Commission has taken in consumer privacy issues relating to mobile apps.

The government transportation official we spoke with said it is very important to identify what data are available to be recorded in an AV, and what are most useful to be recorded. He thought it would be very useful to identify analogous types of data that are gathered by air bags, to resolve uncertainties about what data are useful to understand more about crashes and malfunctions within the car. He acknowledged the public concern over privacy, and the fact that four states have passed legislation concerning EDRs. The legislation identifies data in the EDR as belonging to the owner of the car. He also emphasized the importance of the certifying entity for vehicle communications, noting that the process must not have a significant latency period, which would affect safety. He also queried how an AV is going to be equipped with certificates and how they will be updated.

The media content executive said there needs to be a way to opt out of even anonymized data that are produced by AVs, even data that might have already been collected. He said his legal department is very concerned about privacy, especially relating to location data. He noted that concerns about privacy might be related to demographics: Younger people may be less sensitive. He said that with that demographic, geolocation issues can be handled with a privacy statement. He concluded that there are "no standards yet . . . it's all over the map," and that "It's really the wild west now."

An executive with a global mobile communications provider observed that the standards for how long data should be saved are different in the United States and in Europe, and there are significantly different and often conflicting regulations. He summarized by saying "privacy issues could derail the business."

5. Spectrum and DSRC

One of the global mobile communications providers viewed the communications issue as, "what are the right use cases for spectrum to be used for vehicles?" He proposed that in the early years of AV development, there would be a hybrid approach of communications within the vehicle that would include car owners bringing their own device (like a smartphone), and some services being embedded into the vehicle (e.g., LTE).

An OEM executive concurred with this vision of "embedded vs. tethered" vehicle communications. Like the mobile communications provider, the OEM executive said both embedded and tethered devices would be part of AVs, and also expressed concern about how communications devices in the car would relate to the "driver distraction" problem. The OEM executives stated that OEMs are pretty unanimous in supporting DSRC. However, they explained that there was a lot of concern about reliability and security of DSRC and noted that if all cars have DSRC in the future, the auto industry could get rid of a lot of other safety equipment. They said they would like to see optional regulation concerning DSRC but were not afraid of a government mandate, and estimated that the cost to equip a car with DSRC capability would be approximately $100–$200 per vehicle. When asked about the pending FCC proceeding about opening the 5.9 GHz band to unlicensed devices, the majority of OEM executives stated the AV industry "needs to preserve that frequency." However, one executive asserted that "we are not going to the mat for DSRC."

An AV developer characterized DSRC as "an additional way to provide information to self-driving vehicles." From his company's standpoint, he said, "it's a resource—let's use it."

These thoughts were echoed by a global technology company executive, who explained that it should not be a choice between DSRC and onboard sensors and radars, but rather, an approach to "data diversity," which will improve safety. As a government transportation official characterized it, DSRC would provide the equivalent of a "second opinion" to data obtained by onboard sensors, radar, and lidar. One OEM executive stated that, "we disagree with Google that it should be all onboard technology and communications."

According to another global technology company executive, there needs to be one secure gateway in a car to handle V2V, V2I, and privacy successfully. This gateway needs to have proper protocol layers and be scalable over hundreds of thousands of cars. This executive concurred with the hybrid communications approach expressed by the OEM executives, the government official and the mobile communications provider, and said that once the gateway was in place, there could be a combination of a "mobile phone dongle," an embedded solution, and retrofitting for an aftermarket solution. He agreed that DSRC should be deployed, but that it should not be the only technology for AVs, and added that LTE and other new technologies that could provide data-heavy communications should also play a role. An OEM executive described the need for global harmonization on spectrum and communications issues. He observed that "having to isolate technology makes it difficult to deploy."

An automobile association executive said his organization had not taken a position on DSRC in the current FCC proceeding, but that most of his organization's members believe that spectrum-sharing in the 5.9 GHz (DSRC) band will not work. He commented that if there were a failure in spectrum-sharing technology, it would be extremely difficult to identify the source of the problem and the unlicensed device. Similarly, a Tier 1 supplier offered an analogy between DSRC interference by unlicensed devices and the child's game of Marco Polo, where each blindfolded player tries to locate the other by calling "Marco Polo" back and forth. DSRC allows connected vehicles to identify themselves to each other wirelessly on a continual basis. The supplier compared the interference from unlicensed devices to "a guy with a jackhammer" drowning out the children's calls to locate one another.

Another mobile communications provider said "an autonomous car is still going to be a connected car," and that AVs and connected car technology are developing in parallel. His view was that connectivity is part of the AV experience. In summary, he said spectrum presents a key risk or policy gap for AV development.

6. Other Risks and Policy Gaps

Our interviews identified three other important areas that could inhibit the deployment of AVs: (1) the human/machine interface, (2) standards and regulations, and (3) state laws.

The OEM executives we interviewed were very concerned about how the industry would address the human/machine interface. Specifically, they shared a widespread concern about how to alert a driver that he or she needs to take control back of an AV, perhaps in a matter of seconds. The OEM executives were also concerned about how a "senior" driver was going to interact with complicated new technology.

A global technology company executive was similarly concerned, and pointed out the merging of "infotainment" and "mission critical." A media content expert noted that infotainment is increasingly important for many business models related to AVs. Three of the experts we interviewed discussed the problem of "distracted driving" in the context of "infotainment," and its potential to slow down deployment of AVs into the mass market unless the conflict with state "distracted driving" legislation was resolved.

Another aspect of the human/machine interface challenge is consumer adoption and trust in technology. One of the global technology company executives discussed cultural differences that inform consumer adoption of AVs. She said that in Japan and Korea, there is a positive interest in robotics. In contrast, she said, the United States is generally "robophobic." The Europeans are confident in precision engineering and this provides confidence in precision-engineered vehicles. These consumer attitudes may have a significant impact on AV deployment to the mass market.

A second important issue that could inhibit AV deployment was overly prescribing regulations and standards. An AV developer identified this as a "big concern" and noted that technology does not always evolve in expected directions, which can render regulations and standards obsolete—or, worse, a barrier to development. He added that it was impossible to write relevant standards at this point. A government transportation official said basically the same thing. He examined the possible roles for the government to play, including education and other ways to narrow the focus of disputes. However, when it came to issuing standards, he thought it was extremely difficult to stay relevant, given the swift pace of technological change. He compared government standards to "the elephant sitting on the mouse running a race." Like the AV developer, he also said standards soon become obsolete and retard progress, and that similarly, a government mandate can retard progress.

The third potential inhibitor that was identified was the "50-state problem." OEMs, AV developers, and others we interviewed identified a variety of state factors that may slow mass deployment of AVs. One is different state testing and certification processes for AVs. This would place a very heavy burden on AV developers and OEMs. Another issue concerns state "distracted driving" laws, which differ significantly. These laws may affect the design of screens and displays used within an AV, as well as the use of "infotainment" systems, even when the car is driving itself automatically. Finally, the differences in state tort laws were identified as being a source of concern for deployment of AVs.

D. Conclusions

In summary, our interviews revealed that the following factors: U.S. liability laws, state licensing laws, insurance, privacy protection for data, communications issues, human/machine interface issues, standards and regulations, and other state laws may inhibit the deployment of AVs.

Bibliography

AAA, *Your Driving Costs: How Much Are You Really Paying to Drive?* Heathrow, Fla.: AAA Association Communication, 2013.

Adler, Matthew, "Incommensurability and Cost-Benefit Analysis," *University of Pennsylvania Law Review*, Vol. 146, No. 5, 1998, pp. 1371–1418.

ALI—*See* American Law Institute.

Alonso, William, *Location and Land Use: Toward a General Theory of Land Rent*, Cambridge, Mass.: Harvard University Press, 1964.

American Law Institute, *Restatement of the Law, Second: Torts*, Philadelphia, Pa: 1977.

———, *Restatement of the Law, Third: Torts—Products Liability*, St. Paul, Minn.: American Law Institute Publishers, 1998.

Amend, James M., "GM Links with AT&T to Bring 4G LTE Connectivity in 2014," *WardsAuto*, February 25, 2013. As of August 23, 2013:
http://wardsauto.com/vehicles-amp-technology/
gm-links-att-bring-4g-lte-connectivity-2014

Anderson, James M., "The Missing Theory of Variable Selection in the Economic Analysis of Tort Law," *Utah Law Review*, Vol. 2007, 2007, pp. 255–285.

Anderson, James M., Paul Heaton, and Stephen J. Carroll, *The U.S. Experience with No-Fault Automobile Insurance: A Retrospective*, Santa Monica, Calif.: RAND Corporation, MG-860-ICJ, 2010. As of November 25, 2013:
http://www.rand.org/pubs/monographs/MG860.html

APEC—*See* Asia-Pacific Economic Cooperation.

Applanix, *POS LV 120 Specifications*, October 2012. As of August 13, 2013:
http://www.applanix.com/media/POSLV%20Specs1012.pdf

Arizona State Legislature, HB 2167, 2013. As of August 23, 2013:
http://www.azleg.gov/DocumentsForBill.asp?Bill_Number=2167&Session_
Id=110&image.x=0&image.y=0

Argonne National Laboratory, "The Greenhouse Gases, Regulated Emissions, and Energy Use in Transportation (GREET) Model, GREET 2 2012 rev1," U.S. Department of Energy, 2012. As of August 19, 2013: http://greet.es.anl.gov/

Arieff, Allison, "Driving Sideways," *New York Times*, July 23, 2013. As of August 14, 2013: http://opinionator.blogs.nytimes.com/2013/07/23/driving-sideways/?_r=0

Asia-Pacific Economic Cooperation, Transportation Working Group, Intelligent Transport Systems/Intermodal Experts Group, *World Report for ITS Standards: A Joint APEC-ISO Study of Progress to Develop and Deploy ITS Standards*, Singapore, APEC TPT04/2005, ISO TR 28682, December 2006.

Ayers, David Randal, *Tort Reform and "Smart" Highways: Are Liability Concerns Impeding the Development of Cost-Effective Intelligent Vehicle-Highway Systems?* Charlottesville, Va.: Virginia Transportation Research Council, VTRC 94-R6, March 1994. As of August 14, 2013: http://www.virginiadot.org/vtrc/main/online_reports/pdf/94-R6.pdf

Barth, Matthew, and Kanok Boriboonsomsin, "Traffic Congestion and Greenhouse Gases," *Access*, Vol. 35, Fall 2009, pp. 2–9.

Battelle, *Final Report: Evaluation of the Volvo Intelligent Vehicle Initiative Field Operational Test, Version 1.3*, Washington, D.C.: Federal Highway Administration, U.S. Department of Transportation, January 5, 2007.

Berger, Christian, and Bernhard Rumpe, "Autonomous Driving—Five Years After the Urban Challenge: The Anticipatory Vehicle as a Cyber-Physical System," Braunschweig, Germany: 10th Workshop on Automotive Software Engineering, September 2012, pp. 789–798.

Blincoe, L., A. Seay, E. Zaloshnja, T. Miller, E. Romano, S. Luchter, and R. Spicer, *The Economic Impact of Motor Vehicle Crashes, 2000*, Washington, D.C.: National Highway Traffic Safety Administration, U.S. Department of Transportation, 2002. As of August 19, 2013: http://www.cita-vehicleinspection.org/Portals/cita/autofore_study/LinkedDocuments/literature/NHTSA%20the%20economic%20impact%20of%20motor%20vehicle%20crashes%202000%20USA%202002.pdf

BTS—*See* Bureau of Transportation Statistics.

Buehler, Martin, Karl Iagnemma, and Sanjiv Singh, eds., *The DARPA Urban Challenge: Autonomous Vehicles in City Traffic*, Springer Tracts in Advanced Robotics series, Vol. 56, 2010.

Bureau of Transportation Statistics, "National Transportation Statistics, Table 1-11: Number of U.S. Aircraft, Vehicles, Vessels, and Other Conveyances," Washington, D.C.: Bureau of Transportation Statistics, U.S. Department of Transportation, 2012a. As of August 19, 2013:
http://www.rita.dot.gov/bts/sites/rita.dot.gov.bts/files/publications/national_transportation_statistics/html/table_01_11.html

———, "National Transportation Statistics, Table 1-35: U.S. Vehicle-Miles (Millions)," Washington, D.C.: Bureau of Transportation Statistics, U.S. Department of Transportation, 2012b. As of August 19, 2013:
http://www.rita.dot.gov/bts/sites/rita.dot.gov.bts/files/publications/national_transportation_statistics/html/table_01_35.html

———, *National Transportation Statistics*, U.S. Department of Transportation, July 2013. As of July 29, 2013:
http://www.rita.dot.gov/bts/sites/rita.dot.gov.bts/files/publications/national_transportation_statistics/index.html

Burkhardt, Jon, Arlene Berger, and Adam T. McGavock, "The Mobility Consequences of the Reduction or Cessation of Driving by Older Women," Women's Travel Issues, Second National Conference Proceedings, Washington, D.C.: U.S. Department of Transportation, October 1996. As of August 19, 2013:
http://www.fhwa.dot.gov/ohim/womens/chap22.pdf

Burns, Lawrence D., "Sustainable Mobility: A Vision of Our Transport Future," *Nature*, Vol. 497, No. 7448, 2013, pp. 181–182.

Burns, Lawrence D., William C. Jordan, and Bonnie A. Scarborough, *Transforming Personal Mobility*, New York: The Earth Institute, Columbia University, 2013.

Calabresi, Guido, *The Costs of Accidents: A Legal and Economic Analysis*, New Haven, Conn.: Yale University Press, 1970.

———, "Concerning Cause and the Law of Torts: An Essay for Harry Kalven, Jr.," *University of Chicago Law Review*, Vol. 43, 1975, pp. 69–100.

Calabresi, Guido, and Jon T. Hirschoff, "Toward a Test for Strict Liability in Torts," *Yale Law Journal*, Vol. 81, No. 6, 1972, pp. 1055–1085.

California Vehicle Code, Cal. Veh. Code, Div. 16.6, 2012. As of November 25, 2013:
http://leginfo.legislature.ca.gov/faces/codes_displaySection.xhtml?lawCode=VEH&sectionNum=38750

Carnegie Mellon University, *General Motors–Carnegie Mellon Collaborative Research Labs*, undated. As of August 21, 2013:
http://www.cmu.edu/corporate/partnerships/gm-lab.shtml

Choi, Eun-Ha, Fan Zhang, Eun Young Noh, Santokh Singh, and Chou-Lin Chen, *Sampling Design Used in the National Motor Vehicle Crash Causation Survey*, Washington, D.C.: National Highway Traffic Safety Administration's National Center for Statistics and Analysis, DOT HS 810 930, 2008. As of September 3, 2013:
http://purl.access.gpo.gov/GPO/LPS98147

Christaller, Walter, *Die zentralen Orte in Suddeutschland*, Gustav Fischer, 1933. Translated (in part), by Charlisle W. Baskin, as *Central Places in Southern Germany*, Prentice Hall, 1966.

Coleman, Jules L., *Risks and Wrongs*, Cambridge, UK: Cambridge University Press, 1992.

Colorado General Assembly, SB 13-016, 2013. As of August 21, 2013:
http://www.leg.state.co.us/clics/clics2013a/csl.nsf/billcontainers/F6C2E6A3EE6E F24887257A920050A144/$FILE/016_01.pdf

Cottrell, Nicholas D., and Benjamin K. Barton, "The Role of Automation in Reducing Stress and Negative Affect While Driving," *Theoretical Issues in Ergonomics Science*, Vol. 14, No. 1, 2013, pp. 53–68.

Coxworth, Ben, "Singapore to Try Out Driverless Shuttle on Public Roads," *Gizmag*, August 16, 2013. As of August 28, 2013:
http://www.gizmag.com/singapore-navia-driverless-shuttle/28742/

Cusumano-Towner, Marco, Arjun Singh, Stephen Miller, James F. O'Brien, and Pieter Abbeel, "Bringing Clothing into Desired Configurations with Limited Perception," Shanghai, China: IEEE International Conference on Robotics and Automation (ICRA), 2011. As of August 14, 2013:
http://www.cs.berkeley.edu/~pabbeel/papers/Cusumano-TownerSinghMillerOBrienAbbeel_ICRA2011.pdf

DARPA—*See* U.S. Defense Advanced Research Projects Agency.

Dassbach, Carl H. A., "Where Is North American Automobile Production Headed? Low-Wage Lean Production," *Electronic Journal of Sociology*, Vol. 1, No. 1, 1994. As of September 3, 2013:
http://www.sociology.org/content/vol001.001/dassbach.html

Davis, Stacy C., Susan W. Diegel, and Robert G. Boundy, *Transportation Energy Data Book*, 31st ed., Oak Ridge, Tenn.: Oak Ridge National Laboratory, ORNL-6987, 2012.

Day, John, "Audi Unveils In-Car 4G LTE Wireless Broadband," *John Day's Automotive Electronics*, February 4, 2013. As of August 23, 2013:
http://johndayautomotivelectronics.com/
audi-unveils-in-car-4g-lte-wireless-broadband/

"Dedicated Short Range Communications," Clemson University Vehicular Electronics Laboratory, undated. As of May 20, 2013: http://www.cvel.clemson.edu/auto/systems/dsrc.html

Delucchi, Mark A., "Environmental Externalities of Motor-Vehicle Use in the U.S.," *Journal of Transport Economics and Policy*, Vol. 34, No. 2, 2000, pp. 135–168.

"Desert Race Too Tough for Robots," BBC News, March 15, 2004. As of August 14, 2013: http://news.bbc.co.uk/2/hi/technology/3512270.stm

District of Columbia, *Autonomous Vehicle Act of 2012*, L19-0278, 2013.

DOE—*See* U.S. Department of Energy.

DOE/EPA—*See* U.S. Department of Energy, U.S. Environmental Protection Agency.

Donegal Mutual Insurance v White Consolidated Industries, 166 Ohio App. 3d 569, 2006.

Drews, Frank A., Hina Yazdani, Celeste N. Godfrey, Joel M. Cooper, and David L. Strayer, "Text Messaging During Simulated Driving," *Human Factors*, Vol. 51, No. 5, 2009, pp. 762–770.

EPA—*See* U.S. Environmental Protection Agency.

Exec. Order No. 12291, 46 Fed. Reg. 190, 1981, pp. 13193–13198.

Exec. Order No. 12866, 58 Fed. Reg., 190, 1993, pp. 51735–51744.

Exec. Order No. 13563, 76 Fed. Reg. 14, 2011, pp. 3821–3823.

FCC—*See* Federal Communications Commission.

Federal Communications Commission, "Incentive Auctions: Unleashing Spectrum to Meet America's Demand for Mobile Broadband," fcc.gov, undated a. As of August 23, 2013: http://www.fcc.gov/topic/incentive-auctions

———, "FCC Encyclopedia: Rulemaking Process at the FCC," fcc.gov, undated b. As of August 23, 2013: http://www.fcc.gov/encyclopedia/rulemaking-process-fcc

———, "FCC Allocates Spectrum in 5.9 GHz Range for Intelligent Transportation Systems Uses," Washington, D.C., October 21, 1999. As of August 21, 2013: http://transition.fcc.gov/Bureaus/Engineering_Technology/News_Releases/1999/nret9006.html

———, *Amendment of the Commission's Rules Regarding Dedicated Short-Range Communications Services in the 5.850–5.925 GHz (5.9 GHz Band)*, 19 FCC Rcd 2548, 2004.

————, Report and Order, ET Docket No. 98-95, *Amendment of Parts 2 and 90 of the Commission's Rules to Allocate the 5.850–5.925 GHz Band to the Mobile Service for Dedicated Short Range Communications of Intelligent Transportation Services,* Oct. 21, 2009 (Referring to 1999 Order).

————, "Revision of Part 15 of the Commission's Rules to Permit Unlicensed National Information Infrastructure (U-NII) Devices in the 5 GHz Band," ET Docket No. 13-49, *Notice of Proposed Rulemaking,* 28 FCC Rcd 1769, February 20, 2013. As of June 21, 2013:
http://www.fcc.gov/document/5-ghz-unlicensed-spectrum-unii

Federal Highway Administration, Office of Operations, "Reducing Non-Recurring Congestion," 2013. As of August 14, 2013:
http://ops.fhwa.dot.gov/program_areas/reduce-non-cong.htm

Federal Motor Vehicle Safety Standard 208, Occupant Crash Protection, 1999. As of September 3, 2013:
http://www.nhtsa.dot.gov/cars/rules/import/fmvss/index.html#SN208

Fernandez, Pedro, and Urbano Nunes, "Platooning with IVC-Enabled Autonomous Vehicles: Strategies to Mitigate Communication Delays, Improve Safety and Traffic Flow," *IEEE Transactions on Intelligent Transportation Systems,* Vol. 13, No. 1, 2012, pp. 91–106.

FHWA—*See* Federal Highway Administration.

Fitchard, Kevin, "Is Detroit Buying Verizon's LTE-Connected Car Vision?" *Business Week,* June 7, 2012. As of August 23, 2013:
http://www.businessweek.com/articles/2012-06-07/
is-detroit-buying-verizon-s-lte-connected-car-vision

Florida House of Representatives, CS/HB 1207, 2012. As of August 21, 2012:
http://www.myfloridahouse.gov/Sections/Bills/billsdetail.aspx?BillId=48460

Florida Statutes, Fla. Stat. Title XXIII, Ch. 319, S 145. 2012. As of November 24, 2013:
http://www.flsenate.gov/Laws/Statutes/2012/319.145

FMVSS—*See* Federal Motor Vehicle Safety Standard.

Folsom, Tyler C., "Energy and Autonomous Urban Land Vehicles," *Technology and Society Magazine,* Vol. 31, No. 2, 2012, pp. 28–38.

Ford Motor Company, "Model T Facts," 2012. As of August 16, 2013:
https://media.ford.com/content/fordmedia/fna/us/en/news/2013/08/05/model-t-facts.html

————, *Ford Makes Parallel Parking a Breeze with New Active Park Assist,* 2013. As of August 14, 2013:
https://media.ford.com/content/fordmedia/fna/us/en/news/2011/01/26/ford-makes-parallel-parking-a-breeze-with--new-active-park-assis.html

Funke, G., Gerald Matthews, J. S. Warm, and Amanda K. Emo, "Vehicle Automation: A Remedy for Driver Stress?" *Ergonomics*, Vol. 50, No. 8, 2007, pp. 1302–1323.

Furukawa, Yasutaka, and Jean Ponce, "Accurate Camera Calibration from Multi-View Stereo and Bundle Adjustment," *International Journal of Computer Vision*, Vol. 84, No. 3, 2009, pp. 257–268. As of August 14, 2013: http://link.springer.com/article/10.1007/s11263-009-0232-2#

GAO—*See* U.S. Government Accountability Office.

Garza, Andrew P., "'Look Ma, No Hands!' Wrinkles and Wrecks in the Age of Autonomous Vehicles," *New England Law Review*, Vol. 46, No. 3, 2012, pp. 581–616.

Geier v American Honda Motor Co., 98-1811, 529 U.S. 861, 2000.

Glassbrenner, Donna, *Estimating the Lives Saved by Safety Belts and Air Bags*, Washington, D.C.: National Center for Statistics and Analysis, National Highway Traffic Safety Administration, paper 500, undated. As of September 3, 2013: http://www-nrd.nhtsa.dot.gov/pdf/nrd-01/esv/esv18/CD/Files/18ESV-000500.pdf

Goel, Vindu, "Maps That Live and Breathe with Data," *New York Times*, June 10, 2013. As of August 16, 2013: http://www.nytimes.com/2013/06/11/technology/mobile-companies-crave-maps-that-live-and-breathe.html?_r=0

Google, "Self-Driving Car Test: Steve Mahan," March 28, 2012. As of August 14, 2013: http://www.youtube.com/watch?v=cdgQpa1pUUE

Graham, Kyle, "Of Frightened Horses and Autonomous Vehicles: Tort Law and Its Assimilation of Innovations," *Santa Clara Law Review*, Vol. 52, No. 4, 2012, pp. 1241–1270.

Gurney, Jeffrey K., "Sue My Car, Not Me: Products Liability and Accidents Involving Autonomous Vehicles," unpublished manuscript, 2013. As of August 19, 2013: http://works.bepress.com/cgi/viewcontent.cgi?article=1003&context=jeffrey_gurney

Harrison, Ayodele, and David R. Ragland, "Consequences of Driving Reduction or Cessation for Older Adults," *Transportation Research Record*, Vol. 1843, No. 1, 2003, pp. 96–104.

Hathaway, Oona, "Path Dependence in the Law: The Course and Pattern of Legal Change in a Common Law System," *Iowa Law Review*, Vol. 86, No. 2, 2001.

Hawaii State Legislature, HB 1461, §286, 2013. As of August 21, 2013: http://www.capitol.hawaii.gov/measure_indiv.aspx?billtype=HB&billnumber=1461&year=2013

Hawkins, Troy R., Ola Moa Gausen, and Anders Hammer Strømman, "Environmental Impacts of Hybrid and Electric Vehicles—A Review," *International Journal of Life Cycle Assessment*, Vol. 17, No. 8, 2012, pp. 997–1014.

Hechler, David, "Lost in Translation," *Columbia Law School Magazine*, April 2013, pp. 72–79.

Hensler, Deborah R., M. Susan Marquis, Allan Abrahamse, Sandra H. Berry, Patricia A. Ebener, Elizabeth Lewis, Edgar Lind, Robert MacCoun, Willard G. Manning, Jeannette Rogowski, and Mary E. Vaiana, *Compensation for Accidental Injuries in the United States*, Santa Monica, Calif.: RAND Corporation, R-3999-HHS/ICJ, 1991. As of September 3, 2013: http://www.rand.org/pubs/reports/R3999.html

Highway Loss Data Institute, "Predicted Availability of Safety Features on Registered Vehicles," *Bulletin*, Vol. 28, No. 26, April 2012. As of August 16, 2013: http://www.iihs.org/research/topics/pdf/hldi_bulletin_28.26.pdf

Hill, Kashmir, "GM's Boneheaded Privacy Mistake With OnStar," Forbes.com, September 26, 2011. As of February 9, 2016: http://www.forbes.com/sites/kashmirhill/2011/09/26/gms-boneheaded-privacy-mistake-with-onstar/#24bee3ae7bfc

Hisrich v Volvo Cars of North America, 226 F.3d 445, 6th Cir., August 31, 2000.

Ho, Angela Wei Ling, *Integrating Automobile Multiple Intelligent Warning Systems: Performance and Policy Implications*, thesis, Cambridge, Mass.: Massachusetts Institute of Technology, Engineering Systems Division, Technology and Policy Program, 2006. As of September 3, 2013: http://dspace.mit.edu/handle/1721.1/38571

Hornyak, Tim, "Knife-Wielding Robot HERB Separates Oreo Cookies," *CNET News*, March 12, 2013. As of August 15, 2013: http://news.cnet.com/8301-17938_105-57573865-1/knife-wielding-robot-herb-separates-oreo-cookies/

Houser, Amy, John Pierowicz, and Roger McClellan, *Concept of Operations and Voluntary Operational Requirements for Forward Collision Warning Systems (CWS) and Adaptive Cruise Control (ACC) Systems On-Board Commercial Motor Vehicles*, Federal Motor Carrier Safety Administration, U.S. Department of Transportation, FMCSA-MCRR-05-007, 2005. As of September 3, 2013: http://www.fmcsa.dot.gov/facts-research/research-technology/report/forward-collision-warning-systems.pdf

Houston, David J., and Lilliard E. Richardson Jr., "The Politics of Air Bag Safety: A Competition Among Problem Definitions," *Policy Studies Journal*, Vol. 28, No. 3, August 2000, pp. 485–501.

Hsu, Tiffany, "CES 2013: Lexus Driverless Car: 'Technology Alone Is Not the Answer,'" *Los Angeles Times*, January 7, 2013. As of August 15, 2013:
http://articles.latimes.com/2013/jan/07/autos/
la-fi-tn-ces-hy-lexus-driverless-car-20130107

Hwang, Inseok, Sungwan Kim, Youdan Kim, and Chze Eng Seah, "A Survey of Fault Detection, Isolation, and Reconfiguration Methods," *IEEE Transactions on Control Systems Technology*, Vol. 18, No. 3, 2010, pp. 636–653.

IHRA-ITS—*See* International Harmonized Research Activities Working Group on Intelligent Transport Systems.

IIHS—*See* Insurance Institute for Highway Safety.

Insurance Institute for Highway Safety, "New Estimates of Benefits of Crash Avoidance Features on Passenger Vehicles," *Status Report*, Vol. 45, No. 5, May 20, 2010.

———, "Estimated Time of Arrival," *Status Report*, Vol. 47, No. 1, January 24, 2012.

Intel.com, Intel International Science and Engineering Fair: Winners, 2013. As of August 15, 2013:
http://www.intel.com/content/www/us/en/education/competitions/international-science-and-engineering-fair/winners.html

Intelligent Transportation Society of America, letter to FCC Chairman Julius Genachowski, Washington, D.C., February 12, 2013. As of August 23, 2013:
http://www.itsa.wikispaces.net/file/view/ITS+America+Letter+re+5+9+GHz+Band+and+Connected+Vehicle+Program.pdf

Intelligent Transportation Systems, Joint Program Office, "Connected Vehicle Research," 2013a. As of August 15, 2013:
http://www.its.dot.gov/connected_vehicle/connected_vehicle.htm

———, "Connected Vehicle Research in the United States," 2013b. As of August 23, 2013:
http://www.its.dot.gov/connected_vehicle/connected_vehicle_research.htm

———, "ITS Research Fact Sheets, DSRC: The Future of Safe Driving," 2013c. As of August 21, 2013:
http://www.its.dot.gov/factsheets/dsrc_factsheet.htm

International Harmonized Research Activities Working Group on Intelligent Transport Systems, *Statement of Principles on the Design of High-Priority Warning Signals for In-Vehicle Intelligent Transport Systems*, Geneva: United Nations Economic Commission for Europe, informal document ITS-16-03, October 17, 2008. As of September 3, 2013:
http://www.unece.org/trans/doc/2008/wp29/ITS-16-03e.pdf

International Organization for Standardization, *Intelligent Transport Systems: Lane Departure Warning Systems: Performance Requirements and Test Procedures*, ISO 17361:2007, January 15, 2007a.

———, *Transport Information and Control Systems: Adaptive Cruise Control Systems: Performance Requirements and Test Procedures*, standard 15622, August 23, 2007b.

———, *Transport Information and Control Systems: Forward Vehicle Collision Warning Systems: Performance Requirements and Test Procedures*, standard 15623, 2008a.

———, *Intelligent Transport Systems: Lane Change Decision Aid Systems (LCDAS): Performance Requirements and Test Procedures*, standard 17387, 2008b.

Ioannou, Petros, *Development and Experimental Evaluation of Autonomous Vehicles for Roadway/Vehicle Cooperative Driving*, Berkeley, Calif.: California PATH Research Report UCB-ITS-PRR-98-9, 1998. As of August 15, 2013: http://escholarship.org/uc/item/3q19n51n

ISO—*See* International Organization for Standardization.

James, Robert W., "Absolute Liability for Ultrahazardous Activites: An Appraisal of the Restatement Doctrine," *California Law Review*, Vol. 37, No. 2, 1949, pp. 269–283

Kalra, Nidhi, James M. Anderson, and Martin Wachs, *Liability and Regulation of Autonomous Vehicle Technologies*, Berkeley: California PATH Research Report, UCB-ITS-PRR-2009-28, 2009.

Kelly, Robert B., and Mark D. Johnson, "Defining a Stable, Protected and Secure Spectrum Environment for Autonomous Vehicles," *Santa Clara Law Review*, Vol. 52, No. 4, L. Rev. 1271–1319, 2012.

Kempton, Willett, and Jasna Tomić, "Vehicle-to-Grid Power Fundamentals: Calculating Capacity and Net Revenue," *Journal of Power Sources*, Vol. 144, No. 1, 2005a, pp. 268–279.

———, "Vehicle-to-Grid Power Implementation: From Stabilizing the Grid to Supporting Large-Scale Renewable Energy," *Journal of Power Sources*, Vol. 144, No. 1, 2005b, pp. 280–294.

Koziol, J., V. Inman, M. Carter, J. Hitz, W. Najm, S. Chen, A. Lam, M. Penic, M. Jensen, M. Baker, M. Robinson, and C. Goodspeed, *Evaluation of the Intelligent Cruise Control System*, Washington, D.C.: U.S. Department of Transportation, 1999.

KPMG and Center for Automotive Research, *Self-Driving Cars: The Next Revolution*, 2012.

Kroll, Andrew, "AD Classics: Villa Savoye/Le Corbusier," archdaily.com, 2010. As of August 15, 2013:
http://www.archdaily.com/84524

Lantos, Bâela and Lîorinc Mâarton, *Nonlinear Control of Vehicles and Robots*, London: Springer-Verlag, 2011.

Lee, Douglas B., Lisa A. Klein, and Gregorio Camus, "Induced Traffic and Induced Demand," *Transportation Research Record*, Vol. 1659, 1999, pp. 68–75.

Levin, Doron, "Inside Nissan's $300 Million Battery Factory," CNN Money, 2013. As of August 16, 2013:
http://features.blogs.fortune.cnn.com/2013/04/26/
inside-nissans-300-million-battery-factory/

Li, Shan, "OnStar May Start Selling Data Collected from Cars," *Los Angeles Times*, June 11, 2013. As of August 23, 2013:
http://latimesblogs.latimes.com/technology/2011/09/onstar-privacy-policy.html

Litman, Todd, "Generated Traffic and Induced Travel: Implications for Transport Planning," Victoria, B.C.: Victoria Transport Policy Institute, 2012.

Loh, Edward, "Litigation Assist: Why We Won't Be Getting VW's Lane Assist," Motor Trend Blog, April 16, 2008. As of September 3, 2013:
http://blogs.motortrend.com/6242213/technology/
litigation-assist-why-we-wont-be-getting-vws-lane-assist/18

Mackay, Murray, "Liability, Safety, and Innovation in the Automotive Industry," in Peter W. Huber and Robert E. Litan, eds., *The Liability Maze: The Impact of Liability Law on Safety and Innovation*, Washington, D.C.: Brookings, 1991, pp. 191–223.

Maddox, John, *Improving Driving Safety Through Automation*, presentation at the Congressional Robotics Caucus, National Highway Traffic Safety Administration, July 25, 2012.

Markoff, John, "In Search of a Robot More Like Us," *New York Times*, July 11, 2011. As of August 15, 2013:
http://www.nytimes.com/2011/07/12/science/12robot.html

———, "At High Speed, on the Road to a Driverless Future," *New York Times*, May 27, 2013. As of August 15, 2013:
http://www.nytimes.com/2013/05/28/science/on-the-road-in-mobileyes-self-driving-car.html?pagewanted=all&_r=0

Marchant, Gary E., and Rachel A. Lindor, "The Coming Collision Between Autonomous Vehicles and the Liability System," *Santa Clara Law Review*, Vol. 52, 2012, pp. 1321–1340.

Mashaw, Jerry L., and David L. Harfst, *The Struggle for Auto Safety*, Cambridge: Harvard, 1990.

Massachusetts General Court of the Commonwealth, H 3369, 2013. As of August 21, 2013:
https://malegislature.gov/Bills/188/House/H3369

Martin, Elliot W., and Susan A. Shaheen, *Greenhouse Gas Emission Impacts of Carsharing in North America*, San Jose, Calif.: Mineta Transportation Institute, 2010.

Mathas, Carolyn, "The Burgeoning Use of Sensors for Advanced Driver Assistance Systems," digikey.com, October 20, 2011. As of August 15, 2013:
http://www.digikey.com/us/en/techzone/sensors/resources/articles/the-burgeoning-use-of-sensors.html

McGarity, Thomas O., "Some Thoughts on 'Deossifying' the Rulemaking Process," *Duke Law Journal*, Vol. 41, No. 6, 1992, pp. 1385–1462.

Medford, Ronald, Deputy Administrator of National Highway Traffic Safety Administration, remarks prepared for 51st Annual Workshop on Transportation Law Connected-Driverless Vehicles Panel Session, New Orleans, La., July 17, 2012.

Michalek, Jeremy J., Mikhail Chester, Paulina Jaramillo, Constantine Samaras, Ching-Shin Norman Shiau, and Lester B. Lave, "Valuation of Plug-In Vehicle Life-Cycle Air Emissions and Oil Displacement Benefits," *Proceedings of the National Academy of Sciences*, Vol. 108, No. 40, 2011, pp. 16554–16558.

Michigan Legislature, SB 0169, 2013. As of August 21, 2013:
http://www.legislature.mi.gov/(S(erifeg55ocqewji1byokkuvc))/mileg.aspx?page=getObject&objectname=2013-SB-0169

Montemerlo, Michael, Jan Becker, Suhrid Bhat, Hendrik DahlKamp, Dmitri Dolgov, Scott Ettinger, and Dirk Haehnel, "Junior: The Stanford Entry in the Urban Challenge," *Journal of Field Robotics*, Vol. 25, No. 9, 2008, pp. 569–597. As of August 16, 2013:
http://onlinelibrary.wiley.com/doi/10.1002/rob.20258/abstract

National Coordination Office for Space-Based Positioning, Navigation, and Timing, *Selective Availability*, 2014. As of June 7, 2013:
http://www.gps.gov/systems/gps/modernization/sa/

National Highway Traffic Safety Administration, "U.S. Transportation Secretary Slater Announces Advanced Air Bag Regulation That Improve Benefits and Reduce Risks," press release, U.S. Department of Transportation, Office of Public Affairs, May 5, 2000. As of September 3, 2013:
http://www.nhtsa.gov/About+NHTSA/Press+Releases/2000/U.S.+Transportation+Secretary+Slater+Announces+Advanced+Air+Bag+Regulation+that+Improv+Benefits+and+Reduce+Risks

————, *Special Crash Investigations: Counts of Frontal Air Bag Related Fatalities and Seriously Injured Persons*, Washington, D.C.: U.S. Department of Transportation, National Highway Traffic Safety Administration, National Center for Statistics and Analysis, Crash Investigation Division, January 1, 2008a. As of September 3, 2013:
http://www-nrd.nhtsa.dot.gov/Pubs/AB0108.PDF

————, "Consumer Information: New Car Assessment Program: Notice," *Federal Register*, Vol. 73, No. 134, July 11, 2008b, pp. 40015–40050. As of September 3, 2013:
http://edocket.access.gpo.gov/2008/pdf/E8-15620.pdf

————, U.S. Environmental Protection Agency, California Air Resources Board, *Interim Joint Technical Assessment Report: Light-Duty Vehicle Greenhouse Gas Emission Standards and Corporate Average Fuel Economy Standards for Model Years 2017–2025*, 2010. As of September 3, 2013:
http://www.epa.gov/otaq/climate/regulations/ldv-ghg-tar.pdf

————, *Final Regulatory Impact Analysis: Corporate Average Fuel Economy for MY 2017-MY 2025 Passenger Cars and Light Trucks*, Washington, D.C.: U.S. Department of Transportation, 2012a.

————, *Traffic Safety Facts: Research Note*, Washington, D.C.: U.S. Department of Transportation, 2012b. As of August 23, 2013:
http://www-nrd.nhtsa.dot.gov/Pubs/811701.pdf

————, Preliminary Statement of Policy Concerning Automated Vehicles, released May 30, 2013. As of December 5, 2013:
http://www.nhtsa.gov/About+NHTSA/Press+Releases/U.S.+Department+of+Transportation+Releases+Policy+on+Automated+Vehicle+Development

National Research Council, *Hidden Costs of Energy: Unpriced Consequences of Energy Production and Use*, Washington, D.C.: National Academies Press, Washington, D.C., 2010.

————, *Assessment of Fuel Economy Technologies for Light-Duty Vehicles*, Washington, D.C.: National Academies Press, 2011.

————, *Transitions to Alternative Vehicles and Fuels*, Washington, D.C.: National Academies Press, 2013a.

————, *Review of the Research Program of U.S. DRIVE Partnership: Fourth Report*, Washington, D.C.: National Academies Press, 2013b.

National Transportation Safety Board, *Vehicle- and Infrastructure-Based Technology for the Prevention of Rear-End Collisions*, Washington, D.C., National Transportation Safety Board, 2001. As of September 3, 2013:
http://purl.access.gpo.gov/GPO/LPS24993

NDMV—*See* Nevada Department of Motor Vehicles.

Nebbia, Karl, letter to FCC Chairman Julius Knapp, re FCC ET Docket No 13-49, Revision of Part 15 of the Commission's Rules to Permit Unlicensed National Information Infrastructure (U-NII) Devices in the 5 GHz Band, February 25, 2013.

Neubauer, Catherine, Gerald Matthews, and Dyani Saxby, "The Effects of Cell Phone Use and Automation on Driver Performance and Subjective State in Simulated Driving," Boston: Human Factors and Ergonomics Society Annual Meeting, October 26, 2012, pp. 1987–1991.

Nevada Department of Motor Vehicles, *Adopted Regulation of the Department of Motor Vehicles*, LCB File No. R084-11, 2012. As of August 20, 2013: http://www.leg.state.nv.us/register/RegsReviewed/$R084-11_ADOPTED.pdf

New Hampshire General Court, HB 444, 2013. As of August 21, 2013: http://www.gencourt.state.nh.us/legislation/2013/HB0444.pdf

New Jersey Legislature, A2757, 2012. As of August 21, 2013: http://www.njleg.state.nj.us/2012/Bills/A3000/2757_I1.HTM

New State Ice Co. v Liebman, 285 U.S. 262, March 21, 1932.

New York State Senate, S4912-2013, 2013. As of August 21, 2013: http://open.nysenate.gov/legislation/bill/S4912-2013

Newcomb, Doug, "Sprint Connects with the 2013 Ram Pickup, Dodge Viper," *Wired*, August 10, 2012. As of August 23, 2013: http://www.wired.com/autopia/2012/08/sprint-dodge-ram-uconnect/

NHTSA—*See* National Highway Traffic Safety Administration.

NRC—*See* National Research Council.

NTSB—*See* National Transportation Safety Board.

Obenberger, J., "Managed Lanes," *Public Roads*, Vol. 68, No. 3, 2004, pp. 48–55.

Office of Highway Policy Information, "April 2013 Traffic Volume Trends," U.S. Federal Highway Administration, 2013. As of August 16, 2013: https://www.fhwa.dot.gov/policyinformation/travel_monitoring/tvt.cfm

Office of Management and Budget, *2013 Draft Report to Congress on the Benefits and Costs of Federal Regulations and Unfunded Mandates on State, Local, and Tribal Entities*, Washington, D.C.: Office of Management and Budget, 2013. As of December 6, 2013: http://www.whitehouse.gov/sites/default/files/omb/inforeg/2013_cb/draft_2013_cost_benefit_report.pdf

Ohnsman, Alan, "Tesla CEO Talking with Google about 'Autopilot' Systems," *Bloomberg*, May 7, 2013. As of August 15, 2013: http://www.bloomberg.com/news/2013-05-07/tesla-ceo-talking-with-google-about-autopilot-systems.html

Oklahoma Legislature, HB 3007, 2012. As of August 21, 2013:
http://webserver1.lsb.state.ok.us/cf_pdf/2011-12%20INT/hB/HB3007%20INT.
PDF

Olson, Paul L., Robert Dewar, and Eugene Farber, *Forensic Aspects of Driver Perception and Response*, 2nd ed., Tucson, Ariz.: Lawyers and Judges Publishing Company, 2010.

Oregon State Legislature, HB 2428, 2013. As of November 26, 2013:
https://olis.leg.state.or.us/liz/2013R1/Measures/Overview/HB2428

Owen, David G., John E. Montgomery, and Mary J. Davis, *Products Liability and Safety: Cases and Materials*, 5th ed., New York: Foundation Press, 2007.

Panasonic, "Panasonic Advances Automotive Millimeter-Wave Radar Technology to Detect Pedestrians and Vehicles in Low Visibility Conditions," Osaka, Japan, April 27, 2012. As of August 15, 2013:
http://panasonic.co.jp/corp/news/official.data/data.dir/en120427-2/en120427-2.
html

Parchomovsky, Gideon, and Alex Stein, "Torts and Innovation," *Michigan Law Review*, Vol. 107, No. 2, 2008, pp. 285–316. As of March 18, 2009:
http://www.michiganlawreview.org/archive/107/2/parchomovskystein.pdf

Parry, Ian W.H., Margaret Walls, and Winston Harrington, "Automobile Externalities and Policies," *Journal of Economic Literature*, 2007, pp. 373–399.

Pennsylvania Statute, Title 75, Vehicle Code.

Porcari, John D., letter to Lawrence E. Strickland re FCC ET Docket No 13-49, Revision of Part 15 of the Commission's Rules to Permit Unlicensed National Information Infrastructure (U-NII) Devices in the 5 GHz Band, May 16, 2013.

Poulsen, Kevin, "Hacker Disables More Than 100 Cars Remotely," *Wired*, March 17, 2010. As of August 23, 2013:
http://www.wired.com/threatlevel/2010/03/hacker-bricks-cars/

Priddle, Alisa, and Chris Woodyard, "Google Discloses Costs of Its Driverless Car Tests," *USA Today*, June 14, 2012. As of August 15, 2013:
http://content.usatoday.com/communities/driveon/post/2012/06/google-discloses-costs-of-its-driverless-car-tests/1#.UapgNWRgaBy

Priest, George L., and David G. Owen, "The Invention of Enterprise Liability: A Critical History of the Intellectual Foundations of Modern Tort Law," *Journal of Legal Studies*, Vol. 14, 1985, pp. 461–527.

Public Law 102-240, Intermodal Surface Transportation Efficiency, 1991.

Public Law 106-37, Year 2000 Responsibility and Readiness, 1999.

Public Law 112-96, Middle Class Tax Relief and Job Creation, 2012.

Quain, John R., "Changes to OnStar's Privacy Terms Rile Some Users," *New York Times*, September 22, 2011. As of February 9, 2016:
http://wheels.blogs.nytimes.com/2011/09/22/
changes-to-onstars-privacy-terms-rile-some-users/?_r=0

Raymond, A.E., *Over the Horizon in Air Transportation*, Santa Monica, Calif.: RAND Corporation, P-3396, 1966. As of November 25, 2013:
http://www.rand.org/pubs/papers/P3396.html

Roberts, Stephen N., Alison S. Hightower, Michael G. Thornton, Linda N. Cunningham, and Richard G. Terry, *Advanced Vehicle Control Systems: Potential Tort Liability for Developers*, San Francisco: Nossaman, Guthner, Knox, and Elliot, 1993.

Rosenbloom, Sandra, "Driving Cessation Among Older People: When Does It Happen and What Impact Does It Have?" *Transportation Research Record*, Vol. 1779, 2001, pp. 93–99.

———, "The Travel and Mobility Needs of Older People Now and in the Future," in Joseph F. Coughlin and Lisa A. D'Ambrosio, eds., *Aging America and Transportation: Personal Choices and Public Policy*, New York: Springer, 2012, pp. 39–56.

Ross, H. Laurence, *Settled Out of Court: The Social Process of Insurance Claims Adjustments*, Chicago, Ill.: Aldine Pub. Co., 1980.

SAE—*See* Society of Automobile Engineers.

Samaras, Constantine, and Kyle Meisterling, "Life Cycle Assessment of Greenhouse Gas Emissions from Plug-In Hybrid Vehicles: Implications for Policy," *Environmental Science and Technology*, Vol. 42, No. 9, 2008, pp. 3170–3176.

Schrank, David, Bill Eisele, and Tim Lomax, *TTI's 2012 Urban Mobility Report*, College Station, Texas: Texas A&M Transportation Institute, 2012.

Scott, Michael D., "Tort Liability for Vendors of Insecure Software: Has the Time Finally Come?" *Maryland Law Review*, Vol. 67, No. 2, 2008, p. 425.

Shiau, Ching-Shin Norman, Constantine Samaras, Richard Hauffe, and Jeremy J. Michalek, "Impact of Battery Weight and Charging Patterns on the Economic and Environmental Benefits of Plug-In Hybrid Vehicles," *Energy Policy*, Vol. 37, No. 7, 2009, pp. 2653–2663.

Shoup, Donald C., *The High Cost of Free Parking*, Chicago: Planner's Press, 2005.

Shulman, Mike, and Richard K. Deering, *Third Annual Report of the Crash Avoidance Metrics Partnership, April 2003–March 2004*, Washington, D.C.: National Highway Traffic Safety Administration, U.S. Department of Transportation, DOT HS 809 837, January 2005. As of September 3, 2013:
http://www.nhtsa.gov/DOT/NHTSA/NRD/Multimedia/PDFs/Crash%20
Avoidance/2005/CAMP-IVIThirdAnnualReport.pdf

Siciliano, B., and O. Khatib, *Springer Handbook of Robotics*, Berlin, Germany: Springer, 2008.

Small, Kenneth A., and Camilla Kazimi, "On the Costs of Air Pollution from Motor Vehicles," *Journal of Transport Economics and Policy*, Vol. 29, No. 1, 1995, pp. 7–32.

Smith, Bryant Walker, *Human Factors in Robotic Torts*, unpublished manuscript. As of August 19, 2013:
http://conferences.law.stanford.edu/werobot/wp-content/uploads/sites/29/2013/04/HumanFactorsRoboticTorts_BryantWalkerSmith.pdf

———, *Automated Vehicles Are Probably Legal in the United States*, Stanford, Calif.: Stanford Law School, Center for Internet and Society, 2012a.

———, "Managing Autonomous Transportation Demand," *Santa Clara Law Review*, Vol. 52, 2012b, pp. 1401–1422.

———, "Challenges and Opportunities of Road Vehicle Automation," presented at Transportation Research Board Annual Meeting, San Jose, Calif., July 16, 2013a.

———, "Proximity-Driven Liability," *Georgetown Law Journal*, Vol. 102, September 2013b (working draft; forthcoming 2014).

Society of Automobile Engineers, *Seat Belt Comfort, Fit, and Convenience—Truck and Bus*, standard J1834, 2007.

Society of Automobile Engineers, On-Road Automated Vehicle Standards Committee, *Draft Information Report J3016: Taxonomy and Definitions*, unpublished, 2013.

Society of Automobile Engineers, Safety and Human Factors Steering Committee, *Adaptive Cruise Control (ACC) Operating Characteristics and User Interface*, standard J2399, December 2003a.

———, *Human Factors in Forward Collision Warning Systems: Operating Characteristics and User Interface Requirements*, standard J2400, August 2003b.

Sorensen, Paul, Martin Wachs, Endy M. Daehner, Aaron Kofner, Liisa Ecola, Mark Hanson, Allison Yoh, Thomas Light, and James Griffin, *Moving Los Angeles: Short-Term Policy Options for Improving Transportation*, Santa Monica, Calif.: RAND Corporation, MG-748-JAT/METRO/MCLA, 2008. As of August 15, 2013:
http://www.rand.org/pubs/monographs/MG748.html

South Carolina General Assembly, H 4015, 2013. As of August 21, 2013:
http://www.scstatehouse.gov/sess120_2013-2014/bills/4015.htm

Stanford University, *Volkswagen Automotive Innovation Lab*, undated. As of August 21, 2013:
http://www.stanford.edu/group/vail/

Stevenson, Richard, "Long-Distance Car Radar," *IEEE Spectrum*, September 29, 2011. As of August 15, 2013:
http://spectrum.ieee.org/green-tech/advanced-cars/longdistance-car-radar

Strickland, David L., *The Road Ahead: Advanced Vehicle Technology and Its Implications*, congressional testimony for the U.S. Senate Committee on Commerce, Science, and Transportation, May 15, 2013. As of August 23, 2013:
http://testimony.ost.dot.gov/test/strickland2.pdf

Sunstein, Cass R., "Incommensurability and Valuation in Law," *Michigan Law Review*, Vol. 92, No. 4, 1994, pp. 779–861.

Texas Legislature, HB 2932, 2013. As of August 21, 2013:
http://www.legis.state.tx.us/tlodocs/83R/billtext/pdf/HB02932I.pdf#navpanes=0

Thompson, Kimberly M., Maria Segui-Gomez, and John D. Graham, "Validating Benefit and Cost Estimates: The Case of Airbag Regulation," *Risk Analysis*, Vol. 22, No. 4, August 2002, pp. 803–811.

Thrun, Sebastian, Mike Montemerlo, Hendrik Dahlkamp, David Stavens, Andrei Aron, James Diebel, Philip Fong, John Gale, Morgan Halpenny, Gabriel Hoffmann, Kenny Lau, Celia Oakley, Mark Palatucci, Vaughan Pratt, Pascal Stang, Sven Strohband, Cedric Dupont, Lars-Erik Jendrossek, Christian Koelen, Charles Markey, Carlo Rummel, Joe van Niekerk, Eric Jensen, Philippe Alessandrini, Gary Bradski Bob Davies, Scott Ettinger, Adrian Kaehler, Ara Nefian, and Pamela Mahoney, "Stanley: The Robot That Won the DARPA Grand Challenge," in *The 2005 DARPA Grand Challenge: The Great Robot Race*, Berlin, Germany: Springer, 2007, pp. 1–43. As of August 15, 2013:
http://link.springer.com/chapter/10.1007/978-3-540-73429-1_1

U.S. Census Bureau, *Statistical Abstract of the United States*, Washington, D.C., 2012.

U.S. Code, Title 47, Chapter 5, Communications Act, 1934.

———, Title 42, Chapter 23, Subchapter XIII, §2210, Indemnification and Limitation of Liability, 1957.

———, Title 49, Subtitle VI, Motor Vehicle and Driver Programs, 1966.

———, Title 42, Sections 300aa-1 to 300aa-34, National Childhood Vaccine Injury Act, 1986.

———, Title 33, §2704, Limits on Liability, 1990.

———, Title 5, Chapter 5, Subchapter 2, Administrative Procedure, 1994.

———, Title 15, §6701, Terrorism Risk Insurance Act, 2002.

———, Title 42, §329, Public Readiness and Emergency Preparedness Act, 2005.

———, Title 49, Subtitle VI, Motor Vehicle and Driver Programs, 2006.

U.S. Code of Federal Regulations, Title 49, §1.95(c), Delegations to the National Highway Traffic Safety Administrator, 2010.

U.S. DOT—*See* U.S. Department of Transportation.

U.S. Defense Advanced Research Projects Agency, *The DARPA Grand Challenge 2005*, undated. As of August 14, 2013:
http://archive.darpa.mil/grandchallenge05/gcorg/index.html

U.S. Department of Energy, "eGallon: Compare the Costs of Driving with Electricity," energy.gov, 2013. As of August 19, 2013:
http://energy.gov/articles/egallon-how-much-cheaper-it-drive-electricity

U.S. Department of Energy, U.S. Environmental Protection Agency, fueleconomy.gov home page, 2013. As of August 16, 2013:
http://www.fueleconomy.gov/

U.S. Department of Transportation, Comments to NTIA on FCC NPRM on U-NII Devices in the 5 GHz Band, June 10, 2013.

U.S. Environmental Protection Agency, *Inventory of U.S. Greenhouse Gas Emissions and Sinks: 1990—2011*, Washington, D.C., EPA 430-R-13-001, 2013a. As of August 19, 2013:
http://www.epa.gov/climatechange/Downloads/ghgemissions/US-GHG-Inventory-2013-Main-Text.pdf

———, *Light-Duty Automotive Technology, Carbon Dioxide Emissions, and Fuel Economy Trends: 1975 Through 2012*, Washington, D.C., EPA-420-R-13-001, 2013b. As of September 3, 2013:
http://www.epa.gov/otaq/fetrends.htm

U.S. Government Accountability Office, *ADA Paratransit Services: Demand Has Increased, but Little Is Known About Compliance*, Washington, D.C., GAO-13-17, 2012.

U.S. Interagency Working Group on Social Cost of Carbon, *Technical Support Document: Technical Update of the Social Cost of Carbon for Regulatory Impact Analysis Under Executive Order 12866*, Washington, D.C., 2013. As of August 19, 2013:
http://www.whitehouse.gov/sites/default/files/omb/inforeg/social_cost_of_carbon_for_ria_2013_update.pdf

Urmson, Chris, Joshua Anhalt, Drew Bagnell, Christopher Baker, Robert Bittner, M.N. Clark, Dave Duggins, Tugrul Galatali, Chris Geyer, Michele Gittleman, Sam Harbaugh, Martial Hebert, Thomas M. Howard, Sascha Kolski, Alonzo Kelly, Maxim Likhachev, Matt McNaughton, Nick Miller, Paul Rybski, Bryan Salesky, Young-Woo Seo, Sanjiv Singh, Jarrod Snider, Anthony Stentz, William "Red" Whittaker, Ziv Wolkowicki, Jason Ziglar, Hong Bae, Thomas Brown, Daniel Demitrish, Bakhtiar Litjouhi, Jim Nickolaou, Varsha Sadekar, Wende Zhang, Joshua Struble, Michael Taylor, Michael Darms, and Dave Ferguson, "Autonomous Driving in Urban Environments: Boss and the Urban Challenge," *Journal of Field Robotics*, Vol. 25, No. 8, 2008, pp. 425–466. As of August 16, 2013:
http://onlinelibrary.wiley.com/doi/10.1002/rob.20255/abstract

Urmson, Chris, Charlie Ragusa, David Ray, Joshua Anhalt, Daniel Bartz, Tugrul Galatali, Alexander Gutierrez, Josh Johnston, Sam Harbaugh, Hiroki "Yu" Kato, William Messner, Bryon Smith, Jarrod Snider, Spencer Spiker, Jason Ziglar, William "Red" Whittaker, Michael Clark, Phillip Koon, Aaron Mosher, and Josh Struble, "A Robust Approach to High-Speed Navigation for Unrehearsed Desert Terrain," *Journal of Field Robotics*, Vol. 23, No. 8, 2006, pp. 467–508. As of August 16, 2013:
http://www.ri.cmu.edu/pub_files/pub4/urmson_christopher_2006_1/urmson_christopher_2006_1.pdf

van Wees, Kiliaan A.P.C., "Vehicle Safety Regulations and ADAS: Tensions Between Law and Technology," *2004 IEEE International Conference on Systems, Man and Cybernetics*, Vol. 4, October 10–13, 2004, pp. 4011–4016.

Vandall, Frank J., "Judge Posner's Negligence-Efficiency Theory: A Critique," *Emory Law Journal*, Vol. 35, No. 2, 1986, pp. 383–418.

Velodyne, *High Definition Lidar HDL-64E S2*, Morgan Hill, Calif.: Velodyne Lidar, Inc., 2010. As of August 16, 2013:
http://velodynelidar.com/lidar/products/brochure/HDL-64E%20S2%20datasheet_2010_lowres.pdf

"Velodyne's LiDAR Division Doubles Production Capacity to Meet Demand," *PRWeb.com*, March 11, 2013. As of August 16, 2013:
http://www.prweb.com/releases/2013/3/prweb10512668.htm

von Thünen, Johann Heinrich, *The Isolated State*, Peter Hall, ed., *Von Thünen's Isolated State* (trans., Carla M. Wartenberg), Pergamon Press, 1966.

———, *The Isolated State*, Vol. I, II, and III, 1826, 1850, 1867.

Washington State Legislature, HB 1649, 2013. As of August 21, 2013:
http://apps.leg.wa.gov/billinfo/summary.aspx?bill=1649&year=2013

Wetmore, Jameson M., "Redefining Risks and Redistributing Responsibilities: Building Networks to Increase Automobile Safety," *Science, Technology and Human Values*, Vol. 29, No. 3, 2004, pp. 377–405.

Williamson v Mazda, 131 S.Ct. 1131, 2011.

Wisconsin Legislature, SD 80, 2013. As of August 21, 2013:
https://docs.legis.wisconsin.gov/2013/proposals/sb80

Wood, Stephen P., Jesse Chang, Thomas Healy, and John Wood, "The Potential
Regulatory Challenges of Increasingly Autonomous Motor Vehicles," *Santa Clara
Law Review*, Vol. 52, 2012, pp. 1423–1502.

World Health Organization, *Global Status Report on Road Safety 2013: Supporting
a Decade of Action*, Luxembourg: World Health Organization, 2013. As of August
19, 2013:
http://www.who.int/violence_injury_prevention/road_safety_status/2013/en/
index.html

Wyeth v Levine, 555 U.S. 555, 2009.

Yarrow, Jay, "Human Driver Crashes Google's Self Driving Car," *Business Insider*,
August 5, 2011. As of August 16, 2013:
http://www.businessinsider.com/
googles-self-driving-cars-get-in-their-first-accident-2011-8

Yoo, Christopher S., "Beyond Coase: Emerging Technologies and Property
Theory," *University of Pennsylvania Law Review*, Vol. 160, 2012, pp. 2189–2225.

Zipursky, Benjamin C., "Civil Recourse, Not Corrective Justice," *Georgetown Law
Journal*, Vol. 91, March 2003, pp. 695–756.

Zmud, Johanna, Liisa Ecola, Peter Phleps, and Irene Feige, *The Future of Mobility:
Scenarios for the United States in 2030*, Santa Monica, Calif.: RAND Corporation,
RR-246, 2013. As of December 5, 2013:
http://www.rand.org/pubs/research_reports/RR246.html